lay
ry

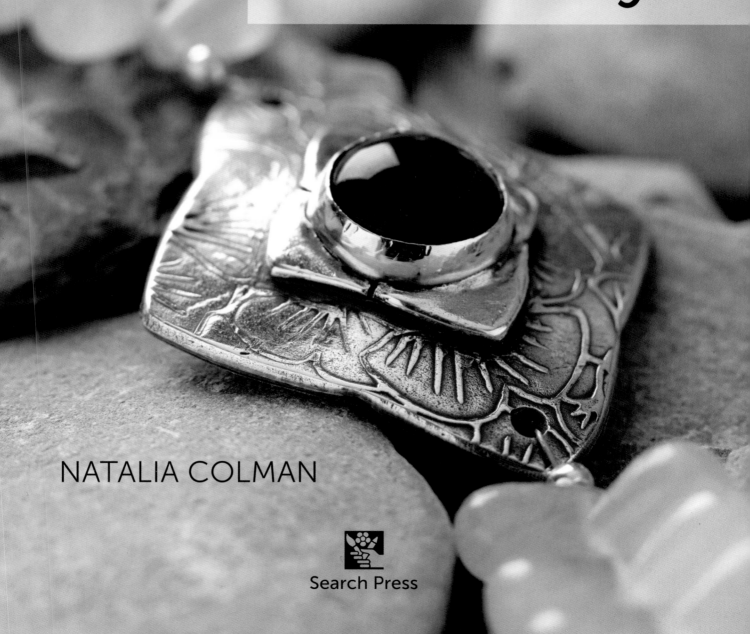

Metal Clay Jewellery

NATALIA COLMAN

Search Press

First published in 2015

Search Press Limited
Wellwood, North Farm Road,
Tunbridge Wells, Kent TN2 3DR

ISBN: 978-1-78221-044-3

The Publishers and author can accept no responsibility for
any consequences arising from the information, advice or
instructions given in this publication.

Suppliers
If you have difficulty in obtaining any of the materials and
equipment mentioned in this book, then please visit the
Search Press website for details of suppliers:
www.searchpress.com

You are invited to visit the author's website:
www.bynatalia.co.uk

Printed in China

Dedication

This book is dedicated to my mother Rosalba
and my daughter Estella, the two most
precious jewels in the world.

Acknowledgements

Getting published was a dream for me, but thank goodness I
chose the perfect publisher to work with. Thank you to
Katie French and Sophie Kersey for your help and support in
getting the structure and content right. A huge thank you to my
editor, Becky Shackleton – your enthusiasm, professionalism and
creative thinking made this a pleasure to write and I learned so
much from you. Thank you to Paul Bricknell for the wonderful
photography and for making the photoshoot so much fun,
and to the design team, in particular Juan Hayward, for
styling the book so perfectly.

I would like to thank Paula Bennett at Jewellery Maker TV
for supplying the metal clay and wonderful gemstones
for the projects.

I do not think I would have got through the epic
process of writing this book if it was not for the support
of my friends Tracey McElroy, Laura Binding and
Hannah Oxberry. Thank you for being so caring and for
checking in on me with late night text conversations.
You really helped me keep going.

Thank you to my beautiful Estella for being so patient
and understanding even when your home was taken over
with full-scale metal clay production for weeks on end.
You never complained and helped me so much;
I could not have done this with without you.

I am deeply grateful to the metal clay community around
the world. Everyone is so pioneering and shares their knowledge
and ideas so generously.

Finally, a special thank you to everyone who has ever attended
one of my workshops, read my books, bought my DVDs or
watched my metal clay shows on JM TV. It is your curiosity,
questions and creativity that drives me to learn, explore and
experiment so I can continue to share it all with you.

Contents

Introduction

I worked for many years as a fashion stylist and even though I love clothes, jewellery is the thing I've always had the greatest fascination with. After years of buying other people's designs but never quite being able to find the exact pieces I was looking for, I decided to learn how to design and make my own. Silver clay was the first jewellery-making medium I began working with.

I discovered it purely by chance while I was researching silversmithing. I was captivated by the idea of creating a piece of precious metal jewellery from an ordinary looking lump of clay that is magically transformed during firing. Since those exciting early days of my foray into jewellery making, advancements in technology have given us an array of different metal clays to work with. Each one of them has its own beautiful properties and requires slightly different methods for handling and firing.

Through the techniques and projects in this book I hope to show you the incredible potential of silver, copper and bronze clays, and demonstrate how a few simple processes can transform them into beautiful pieces of jewellery. All of the projects can be fired with a gas torch, or using a gas hob in the case of silver clay, so they are easy to get started with if you are a newcomer to the world of metal clay. If you already have experience of working with metal clays, I hope to inspire you with some fresh techniques and design ideas for these unique and very beautiful precious materials.

Clays

Precious metal clays all consist of the same components: tiny particles of precious metal held together with water and a special binding medium. Metal clay can be moulded, rolled, shaped, sculpted and carved in exactly the same way as ceramic clay but the difference is, when the water has evaporated from the clay and it is fired at the right temperature for the right length of time, the particles melt together to form a piece of solid precious metal. Pure magic!

Silver clay

I always think of silver clay as the jewel in the crown of the metal clay range. Silver is one of the noble metals – metals that are resistant to corrosion and oxidisation in moist air and regarded as most precious due to their rarity. It is certainly the easiest of all the metal clays to work with. It was invented in Japan in 1990 and was the first precious metal clay to revolutionise silver jewellery making. In the early days it could only be fired in a kiln and after firing, the clay shrank by 30 per cent. Continuous research and development by the manufacturers of the clay has meant that the silver clay products we use today can be fired with a kiln, gas torch or on a gas stove and they shrink by just 6–8 per cent. After firing, silver clay pieces have a silver content of 99.9 per cent, unlike sterling silver which has a 92.5 per cent silver content. Pieces made from silver clay are referred to as 'fine silver'. In the UK it is a legal requirement to hallmark any individual piece of silver that is sold above the weight of 7.78g ($^1/_3$ oz). The Assay Office will stamp fine silver pieces with a hallmark of 999.

SILVER CLAY MANUFACTURERS

At the time of writing this book, there are two main manufacturers of silver clay, both of whom are Japanese. Mitsubishi Materials, the original inventors of silver clay who manufacture products called PMC (Precious Metal Clay), and Aida Industries, whose range of silver clay products are sold under the brand name Art Clay Silver. For ease of explanation, all the projects in this book have been made using Art Clay Silver. The firing times and temperatures table on pages 138–139 includes instructions for both PMC and Art Clay Silver.

LUMP CLAY

The main type of clay used in this book is known as 'lump clay'. Lump clay is a wonderful medium because it can be modelled just like ceramic clay. You can use tools to roll and shape it or sculpt it with your hands. You can also add water to the clay to make it softer and more malleable. Once it has dried out, it can be easily shaped, carved, sanded and refined before it is fired.

PASTE CLAY

Paste clay is a watered-down version of lump clay and has the consistency of melted ice cream. It is perfect for sticking two pieces of clay together before firing, in the same way that slip (watery clay) would be used when working with ceramic clay. Paste clay is excellent for use as a decoration or can be painted onto organic objects such as leaves, petals and twigs. After the paste has dried, the object can be fired and will burn away, leaving a beautiful silver replica in its place. You can create your own paste by watering down lump clay or adding water to bits of leftover or dried-out clay.

SYRINGE CLAY

Syringe clay is a stiffer version of paste clay and comes pre-loaded in a syringe. You can add different tips to the syringe and extrude the clay to create decorative effects, in the same way as you would use piped icing.

It is also useful for sealing joins between pieces of clay because you can apply the clay very precisely using the syringe. The syringe is also an excellent tool for creating very fine, filigree-style pieces. Once opened, you can keep the syringe clay hydrated by standing it nozzle-end down in a cup of water.

9

Copper and bronze clay

Copper has been an essential material to man since prehistoric times and has played an important role in many civilizations, including the Ancient Egyptians and the Romans – it may well be the oldest metal in use, as copper artefacts dating to 8700 BCE have been discovered. Bronze is also a very ancient metal and dates back to around 4000 BCE – bronze sculptures and jewellery dating from this time have been discovered at sites in China and Mesopotamia. There's something wonderful about creating jewellery using a material discovered by our ancient ancestors but giving it a modern twist.

Copper and bronze clays came about due to the inventiveness of American artist and metallurgist Bill Struve. His early career in chemistry and engineering gave him the skills and initiative to develop a process for recycling copper and combining it with water and a non-toxic binding material to create copper clay. While silver clays can be fired in a relatively simple and quick way, copper is a much trickier metal to deal with in clay form. Copper and bronze – which is 90 per cent copper – react to oxygen when they are hot and the metal oxidises. This creates a thick red-brown crust on the metal known as firescale, which can be very hard to remove. Struve invented his own brand of copper and bronze clays and discovered that kiln firing the pieces buried in activated coconut carbon in a metal box, eradicated the oxidisation. This was a major breakthrough for metal clays and over the years has led to the creation of the rapid and low-fire clays that are on the market today.

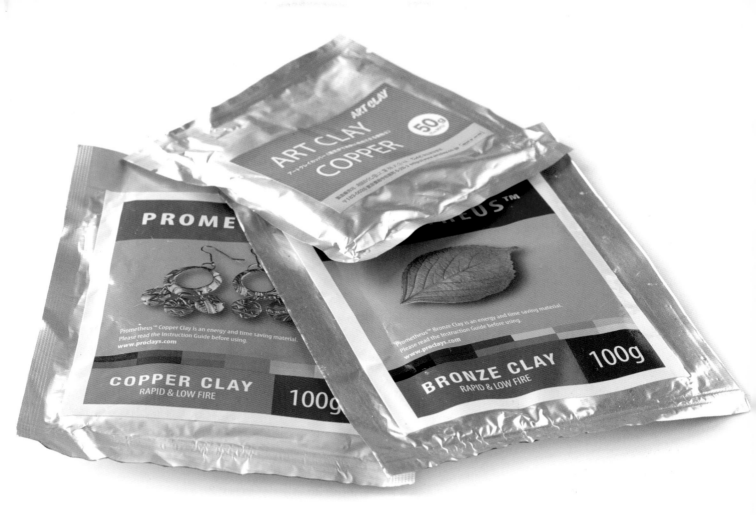

COPPER CLAY

There are a variety of different brands of copper clay available, many of which need to be kiln fired for between two to five hours. Creating jewellery in this way is an expensive and lengthy process, so it has been exciting to see some new rapid and low-fire clays arrive on the market. All the copper pieces in this book have been made using Prometheus copper clay. The firing chart on pages 138–139 gives guideline times and temperatures for both Prometheus copper clay and Art Clay copper. Prometheus clay was developed by Turkish kiln manufacturers Odak Industries and is one of the few copper clays that can be fired for a relatively short amount of time in a kiln or with a gas torch; copper clay needs a higher firing temperature than silver clay and it cannot be fired on a gas stove. While low-fire clays can be fired using a gas torch, there is still the danger

of oxidisation when the hot copper begins to cool and reacts with oxygen. When torch firing, it is important that you quench the fired piece immediately in cold water before it begins to cool. This will significantly reduce the amount of firescale on your pieces.

BRONZE CLAY

Bronze clay is a combination of two metals: it is 90 per cent copper and 10 per cent tin. Although it has a high copper content, it takes on a golden appearance after it has been fired – I also find that Prometheus bronze clay has a slightly duller finish than the copper clay. It still looks beautiful, but a little more rustic. All of the projects using bronze clay in this book have been made with Prometheus bronze clay.

11

Basic equipment

Whether you are working with silver, copper or bronze clay there is certain equipment that you will use time and time again. Here are some of the items that I cannot live without.

PLASTIC FOOD WRAP

This simple piece of equipment is a necessity when working with metal clays: you can knead the clay while it is covered in plastic wrap, to condition it and prevent it from sticking to your hands, and it can be used to prevent excess clay from drying out. It is best to store the plastic-wrapped clay inside a screw-top jar or airtight container along with a wet baby wipe to create a moist atmosphere, so that the clay remains hydrated between uses.

MODELLING CLAY

It is a good idea to first create a version of your design using modelling or polymer clay – you can see how the design will look and work out how much metal clay you will need.

CLAY BALM

It is essential to add a thin layer of clay balm to your rolling pin and rolling surface – I like to use a square of teflon – as well as any cutters and texture mats you use. Choose a balm that has been specially formulated for use with metal clays – these products tend to contain ingredients such as natural oils, beeswax and cocoa butter. Alternatively, olive oil is perfect for using as a resist on your work surface and hands. Avoid using petroleum-based balms as they can react adversely with the binding agents in the metal clays.

TEXTURE STAMPS

One of the greatest advantages metal clays have over sheet metal is that you can add texture and pattern to them with ease. A huge range of rubber and plastic texture sheets are made especially for use with metal and polymer clays and they are well worth investing in.

BABY WIPES

I always keep a pack of baby wipes to hand as they are perfect for cleaning the metal residue from your hands, tools and work surfaces. They are also very useful for helping to refine dried clay. Rub a damp baby wipe along the edges of your dried clay pieces to give a smooth and silky finish to the clay.

HOLE-MAKING TOOLS

You will sometimes need to cut holes in your metal clay, either for attaching findings or for decoration. You can use everyday items such as drinking straws and cocktail sticks to do this while the clay is wet; a pin vice is ideal for use on dried, unfired clay; while a drill can be used for fired metal clay.

ROLLING TOOLS

The two items I use most frequently when I'm working are a mini rolling pin and a snake roller – a small clear square of perspex. The rolling pin will help you to roll clay to even thicknesses, while a snake roller will help you roll perfectly even ropes of clay (see page 80). You may need to use liquid glycerine or water to condition your clay before you roll it.

PLAYING CARDS

I like to use playing cards to keep my clay level and at a specific thickness when I roll it out. Simply place the required number of cards on either side of your clay before you roll – keeping the ends of the rolling pin on top of the cards will ensure that the clay does not become thinner than the depth of the cards (see page 17). One playing card is equivalent to 1mm ($1/16$ in); tape the cards together to prevent them from moving around when rolling out. There are alternatives, such as plastic slats of varying thicknesses and clay rolling frames.

CUTTING TOOLS

Once you have rolled out your metal clay you will need to cut it. You can buy cutters in a wide assortment of shapes and sizes – cookie cutters or sugarcraft cutters can be ideal. However, there will also be times when you will want to cut a particular shape for which a standard cutter does not exist. For geometric shapes you will need a tissue blade – a straight, fine blade – and for more complex templates a fine needle tool is essential.

FIRING TOOLS

Most important of all is the equipment you will need to fire your metal clay pieces. There is some general equipment that you will need for any method of firing, such as protective goggles, long tweezers or tongs, and a metal tray or heat-resistant container of water for quenching hot pieces of fired metal. But there are three ways you can fire your pieces, and this is what you will need:

For gas stove firing:
• Gas stove
• Piece of heat-proof wire mesh

For kiln firing:
• Kiln: you will need a kiln that reaches the following minimum temperatures: 650°C (1202°F) for silver clay; 820°C (1508°F) for bronze clay; 900°C (1652°F) for copper clay
• Fibre blanket to support your pieces during firing
• Steel box with lid, for copper and bronze pieces
• Active coconut shell carbon or magic carbon, for copper and bronze pieces

PAINTBRUSH

A paintbrush is useful for sealing joins, applying paste, smoothing any imperfections on your clay and for working with ropes of clay to create coils. It is worth having varying sizes of paintbrush at your disposal, depending on the size of the piece you are working on and the amount of detailed work you are doing. Always clean your brushes after use.

WIRE BRUSH

When your pieces of metal clay have been fired they will have a dull finish – you will need to use a wire brush to remove the surface layer and bring out the beautiful shiny qualities of the metal. It is worth investing in a brass or fine wire brush for each type of clay you are using and keeping those brushes separate so that you don't contaminate your different metals.

AGATE BURNISHER

This tool is a piece of agate mounted onto a bamboo handle and is used to burnish the surface of the metal clay to flatten it and create a high shine. It is particularly effective for polishing the edges of pieces and any piece that has a close texture. It is not recommended for plain pieces or for use on large, flat areas of metal because it can scratch the surface.

METAL POLISH

Metal polish is perfect for creating a mirror-like finish on fired pieces of metal clay. Use a cloth or paper towel to apply a small amount of metal polish and use a soft cloth to clean the polish away and to buff the surface of the metal.

SANDING MATERIALS

You will need to use different gradients of sanding sponges to smooth and refine your clay pieces before firing. Begin by using the coarsest grade first, working your way down to the finest. The more neatly you finish your pieces before firing the better they will look after firing. Remember, it is much easier to sand and smooth the dry clay than it is to file the fired metals.

For gas torch firing:

- Jewellers' gas torch: use a small torch for firing silver clay because this can be fired at a temperature of between 650–800°C (1202–1472°F). Use a larger, hotter torch for firing copper and bronze clay because these metals need to be fired at a temperature of 820°C (1508°F) for bronze clay, and 900°C (1652°F) for copper clay
- Butane-propane gas mixture
- Firing block

remember

After firing, you will need to place your copper and bronze pieces in a pickle solution to remove any firescale. A small slow cooker is the ideal receptacle for pickling your metal clay pieces. It will maintain a gentle heat and has a lid to prevent the solution from evaporating. You could also place the pickle solution in a lidded thermal cup flask, or use a saucepan to gently heat the pickle solution. Be sure to place a lid over it and keep it at a very low heat. Do not use these receptacles for foodstuff.

Techniques

In this section I will guide you through the important techniques you will use time and time again when working with metal clays. We will look at how to get started; handling and storing your clay once you have opened it; drying; reconstituting dried-out clay; and most importantly – how to fire your different metal pieces.

Silver clay

Of all the metal clays, silver clay is the easiest to handle and the simplest and quickest to fire. New formulations of silver clay have brought us a product that has a relatively long working time and is easy to rehydrate. I would always advise anyone who is new to metal clays to start with silver clay, as it is quite simply the easiest and most beautiful to work with. The following techniques form the basis of many of the projects and will help you achieve great results every time.

top tip

Have a design in mind before you open a packet of silver clay. Work out the design detail first using modelling or polymer clay to see how it will look and work out how much clay you will need.

PREPARING

1 Plan your design and gather together all the tools and materials you will need before you open your packet of clay. Trust me – preparation is key! Ensure that all of your equipment has been cleaned thoroughly to remove all traces of other metal clays to avoid cross-contamination. Use a baby wipe or damp cloth to clean them if need be.

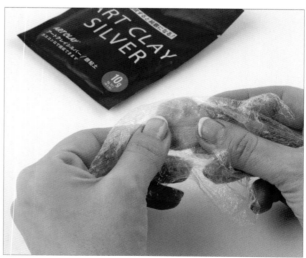

2 Remove your silver clay from its packaging and place it inside some plastic wrap. Knead the clay for a minute or two to soften it and make it malleable. Only take out as much clay as you need, to minimise waste.

ROLLING

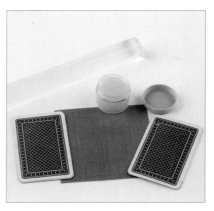

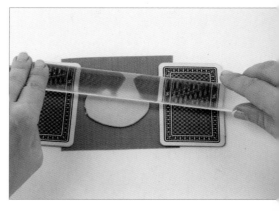

1 Decide how thick you want to roll your clay and tape together two sets of playing cards of the corresponding thickness. For a standard piece it is advisable to roll the clay to a thickness of five playing cards so that the silver is strong when fired.

2 Add a thin layer of clay balm or olive oil to your work surface and rolling pin. Place a set of playing cards on each side of your work surface.

3 Place the silver clay between the playing cards and roll it out, turning it occasionally, until you have achieved the shape you want. The playing cards will ensure that the clay is an even depth all over and will prevent you from rolling it too thinly.

HANDLING

Rub a little clay balm or olive oil onto your hands when handling the clay. This will prevent it from sticking to your fingers. If the clay dries out while you are working with it, simply add a drop or two of water and knead the clay to bring it back to a soft and workable state.

STORING UNUSED CLAY

Once opened, silver clay will need to be stored in moist conditions or it will dry out. Tightly wrap any unused clay in plastic wrap and place inside a screwtop jar or airtight container. Add a wet baby wipe or a wet piece of cloth to the container – this will create a moist environment and ensure that the clay stays hydrated.

Unopened packets of silver clay have a shelf life of up to five years, so do not panic if you have bought some clay and not used it. Store unopened packets in a cool dark place. Do not refrigerate or freeze.

Bronze and copper clay

Copper clay is 99.9 per cent copper after firing and bronze clay contains 90 per cent copper and 10 per cent tin, so both of these metal clays perform in a very similar way when you are working with them. Prometheus copper clay has a fairly crumbly consistency so needs to be conditioned well before using. Art Clay copper and Prometheus bronze clay are beautifully soft and can be used straight from the packet.

PREPARING

1 Ensure that all of the tools and equipment you are using have been cleaned thoroughly to remove all traces of other metal clays to avoid cross-contamination. Use a baby wipe or damp cloth to clean them off.

2 Only take as much clay out of the packet as you need to work with. This is a good general rule to abide by, but especially if you are working with bronze, as it will begin to oxidise and discolour if it stays out in the open air.

top tip
Bronze and copper clay pieces fired with a small gas torch (up to 900°C/1652°F) should be no larger than 3cm (1¼in) and no thicker than 4mm (⅛in). If you would like to torch fire pieces larger than this you will need to use a larger, hotter torch (up to 1500°C/2732°F). If you are firing your pieces in a kiln then you can make a piece any size you wish as long as it will fit inside your kiln space.

ROLLING

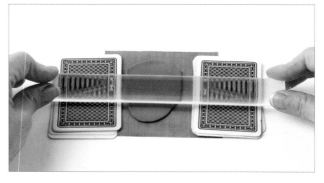

1 To prevent the clay sticking, add a thin layer of clay balm or olive oil to your work surface and rolling pin.

2 When you have chosen your thickness, place the requisite number of playing cards on either side of your clay. The playing cards will keep the clay an even depth as you roll, and prevent you from rolling too thinly.

HANDLING

It is advisable to apply a barrier cream to your hands before handling bronze or copper clay. The binding ingredients in the clay are non-toxic, but the clay itself can occasionally irritate and stain the skin. I strongly advise you to wash your hands or at least wipe them with a baby wipe after handling the clay to avoid ingesting the metal particles and to avoid staining your skin and fingernails. If you prefer you may wish to wear latex gloves when working with the clay.

STORING UNUSED CLAY

Wrap any unused bronze and copper clay in plastic wrap and place it inside a screwtop jar or airtight container. Add a wet baby wipe or a wet piece of cloth to the container – this will create a moist environment and ensure that the clay stays hydrated.

Metal clay that remains unopened in its packaging has a shelf life of up to five years so there is no rush to use up your unopened clay. Store unopened packs in a cool dark place. Do not refrigerate or freeze.

CONDITIONING

Bronze and copper clays are not as naturally silky as silver clay, and may need softening up if they have dried out in storage. Condition them by adding a few drops of liquid glycerine or water and knead for a few minutes inside a piece of plastic wrap. The texture of the clay needs to be smooth and supple; if, after kneading, it still looks crackly or lumpy, you may need to add a little more water or glycerine and knead for a few more minutes.

Drying metal clay

Before you fire any pieces of metal clay you must ensure that they are completely dry. Any moisture that remains in the piece when it is fired will cause the metal to crack or blister – as the metal heats up the moisture will work its way towards the surface as it tries to escape. To check if the clay is completely dry, put the hot clay (straight from drying) on a cold mirror. After 10–20 seconds, move it and check that there is no condensation on the mirror. This test is especially important for large and thick pieces. If you are in any doubt as to whether a piece has had long enough to dry, err on the side of caution – be patient and fire it at a later stage.

The following table gives guideline times for metal clays based on a test piece weighing 5g ($^1/_5$oz). The hair dryer referred to in the chart is 1200w, held 3–5cm (1¼–1¾in) away from the piece of metal clay. These are the minimum recommended drying times. Extend the drying time if a larger amount of clay is used or if any additional liquid is added to the clay.

top tip

There are no time limits for firing dried pieces of metal clay. Simply store the pieces at room temperature in a dry place where they won't get knocked or damaged, until you are ready to fire them.

METAL CLAY PRODUCT	ROOM TEMPERATURE	HAIR DRYER	HOT PLATE, OVEN, KILN OR FOOD DEHYDRATOR
ART CLAY SILVER 650	24 hours	15 minutes	10 minutes at 150°C (320°F)
ART CLAY COPPER	24 hours	20–30 minutes	1 hour at 150°C (320°F)
PMC +	24 hours	15–30 minutes	15–30 minutes at 150°C (320°F)
PMC 3	24 hours	15–30 minutes	15–30 minutes at 150°C (320°F)
PROMETHEUS BRONZE	24 hours	20–30 minutes	1 hour at 150°C (320°F)
PROMETHEUS COPPER	24 hours	20–30 minutes	1 hour at 150°C (320°F)

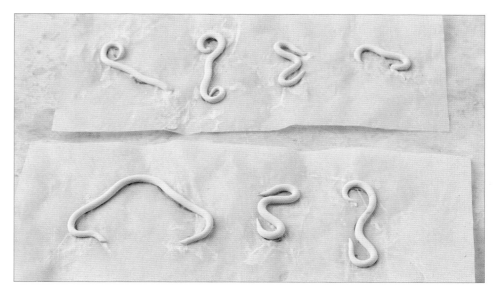

DRYING AT ROOM TEMPERATURE

The easiest drying method is to leave your pieces to dry naturally at room temperature – just make sure you put them somewhere they won't get damaged, either on a piece of greaseproof paper or on your teflon working surface.

DRYING WITH HEAT

A hot plate, such as the one shown here, is an excellent way to dry your pieces in a relatively short amount of time. Be careful when handling your pieces once they're dried, as the surface will get very hot. Alternatively, use a hair dryer to dry your pieces faster than at room temperature.

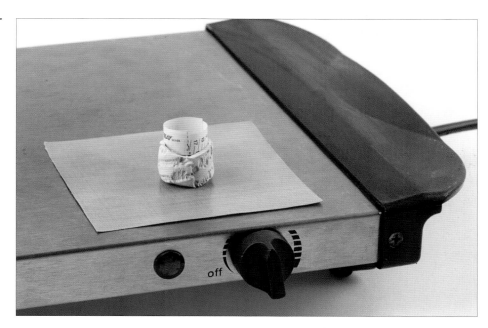

top tip

If you don't own a hot plate or dehydrator, there are a number of different options to speed up the drying process. Place your clay pieces on a teflon sheet on a baking tray and put them into a cool oven. Keep the temperature no higher than 80°C (176°F) because you do not want the binder to burn away. You can also use a mug warmer: place the pieces inside an airing cupboard or on top of a radiator – anywhere that is warm and dry.

Reconstituting metal clay

One of the challenges of working with metal clays is that they can dry out quite quickly while you are working with them or when they are not in use. While there is nothing quite as good as clay that is brand new and fresh out of the packet, here are a few steps you can follow to bring your metal clay back to a workable state.

IF YOUR CLAY HAS A CRACKED APPEARANCE...

If your clay has begun to dry out and takes on a cracked appearance while you are working with it, simply add a couple of drops of water, place it in some plastic wrap and knead it for a few minutes to work the moisture back into the clay. You may want to use a few drops of liquid glycerine with copper and bronze clay, instead of water.

IF STORED CLAY IS TOO DRY TO WORK WITH...

If excess clay you have stored has become too dry work with, poke a few holes in the surface of the clay then cut it into smaller chunks. Add a little water and knead the clay pieces. Place the clay in a screwtop jar or airtight container along with a wet baby wipe or piece of wet cloth. Ensure that the clay and cloth or baby wipe are not touching. Leave the clay to rehydrate for 24 hours then knead it back into a workable state. If the clay has become wet or sticky, allow it to air dry for a few minutes before use.

IF YOUR CLAY HAS DRIED OUT COMPLETELY...

If your clay pieces have dried out completely, or you make a design that you decide you don't want to fire, it is possible to reconstitute the dried pieces back into lump clay by grinding them up and rehydrating them. Simply follow the steps given below.

1 Place the pieces of dried-out clay in a mortar. Use a pestle to grind the clay into a fine powder.

2 Wrap a piece of hosiery tightly over a small container (7–10 denier stockings work well for this purpose).

3 Place the ground clay powder on top of the hosiery, which will act like a sieve. Use a small brush to push the powder through into the container.

4 The powder will pass easily through the hosiery and any lumps of clay will remain on the top. Return the lumps of clay to the mortar and grind them again. Repeat steps 1–3 as necessary until all the clay passes through.

5 Remove the hosiery and add some water to the clay powder a drop at a time.

6 Use a palette knife to bind the powder and water together and reconstitute the mixture back into lump clay. If the clay becomes too sticky, allow it to air dry for a few minutes before kneading and re-using.

Firing silver clay

When metal clays are fired to the correct temperature, the binding ingredient burns away and the metal particles melt together. This process is known as sintering. Silver clay has the simplest and quickest firing process of all the metal clays (see pages 138–139 for firing times and temperatures). Small silver clay pieces can be fired in as little time as two minutes, which makes working with this precious metal a pure luxury. Silver clay can be fired using three methods: using a kiln, with a gas torch or on a gas stove. All three methods are very effective and result in the same outcome – a strong piece of fine silver.

FIRING WITH A GAS TORCH

This method of firing puts you in control of directing the heat, so you need to stay alert and be careful not to overheat and melt the silver. This is the quickest method of firing so do not be discouraged by the idea of working with a live flame. Art Clay Silver 650, PMC+ and PMC 3 silver clay products can be fired with a gas torch. This method is best for pieces weighing up to 25g (1oz) and no larger than 5 x 5 x 2cm (2 x 2 x ¾in). Cubic zirconia and certain gemstones up to 5mm (½in) are safe to be fired using this method.

warning!

Do not fire metal pieces containing glass or ceramics with a gas torch because the instant intensity of heat will crack or shatter them.

warning!

Tie long hair back and ensure you have no loose articles of clothing that could come into contact with the flame. Wear a pair of protective goggles.

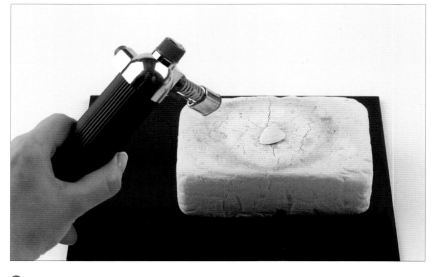

2 Ignite the gas torch and direct the flame towards the metal clay at a 45-degree angle. Hold the torch at a distance of around 5cm (2in).

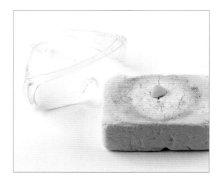

1 Place the dried silver clay piece on the centre of a fire-resistant block.

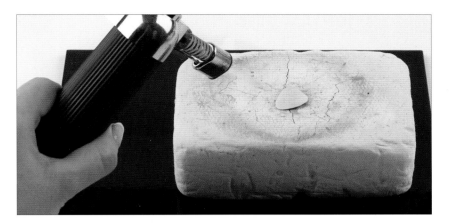

top tip

If the piece begins to shimmer or looks glossy this means it has become too hot and is beginning to melt. Direct the flame away from the piece for a couple of seconds and slowly bring the flame back towards the piece until it glows a peach colour once more.

3 Slowly move the flame over the piece to heat it evenly. You will see a little smoke and flame as the binder burns away. When the piece begins to glow a peach colour, start to time the firing. Turn the lights off in the room so that you can see the colour of the hot metal. Continue to heat for the recommended length of time (according to the instructions on pages 138–139).

4 Allow the piece to cool naturally or use metal tongs to pick up the piece and quench it in cold water. Do not quench pieces that contain glass, gemstones, cubic zirconia or ceramics – as the swift change in temperature can cause them to shatter – allow these to cool naturally.

top tip

If you are planning to add gold leaf to your piece don't quench it after firing. Quenching the silver clay makes the surface more porous. When you apply gold leaf to silver you will heat up the silver so that the gold leaf can melt onto the surface. If the piece is too porous the gold leaf can disappear through the minute holes in the surface.

KILN FIRING

A kiln allows you to fire bigger pieces with no restrictions on the weight of the clay. If you want to make projects containing large quantities of organic materials, or that contain glass or ceramics, then a kiln is the best option for you.

1 Place the dried silver clay piece on a kiln shelf or piece of fibre blanket and use long-handled metal tongs to place it inside the kiln. For large, complex pieces such as the mermaid pendant (pages 82–87) use the fibre blanket to support the shape of the clay so that it doesn't warp.

2 Close the door and set the kiln to the required temperature – see pages 138–139 for firing temperatures and times. Do not start to time the firing until the kiln has reached the required temperature. After the firing time has been reached, turn off the kiln.

top tip

You can pre-heat the kiln to the required temperature and then place your pieces inside. Alternatively, you can place your pieces inside a cold kiln and allow it to heat up. Begin timing the firing only when you kiln has reached the required temperature.

3 You can allow the pieces to cool inside the kiln by opening the door and leaving it ajar, or you can remove the shelf or fibre blanket from the kiln using metal tongs and place the piece on a heat-resistant surface. If you don't want to wait for the silver to cool naturally, you can quench it – simply use the tongs to submerge the piece in cold water. Do not quench pieces containing glass, gemstones, cubic zirconia or ceramics.

FIRING ON A GAS STOVE

Art Clay Silver and PMC 3 can be fired on a gas stove. This method is best for pieces weighing up to 30g (1oz) and no larger than 5 x 5 x 2cm (2 x 2 x ¾in). Projects that contain gemstones no larger than 5mm (¼in) can also be fired using this method. Pieces containing glass or ceramics should not be fired on a gas stove.

1 Place a piece of stainless steel mesh on a gas stove. Turn on and light the gas.

top tip

Turn off the room lights during firing so that you can see the colour of the silver clay piece more clearly.

2 Place your silver clay piece on the mesh where it is glowing brightest. You will see a flame and some smoke as the binder burns away. Wait until the silver clay piece glows a rosy peach colour – the colour it turns when at optimum heat – then set a timer.

3 After firing, allow the piece to cool before handling or use some metal tongs to pick up the piece and quench it in cold water. Do not quench pieces that contain gemstones or cubic zirconia – allow these to cool naturally.

Firing bronze and copper clay

Bronze and copper clays need to be fired at a higher temperature than silver clay (see pages 138–139 for firing times and temperatures). This means that gas stove firing is not an option for bronze and copper clay pieces as it does not produce high enough temperatures. The additional challenge when firing copper and bronze clays is to minimise oxidisation. If the metal oxidises during firing a reddish-brown crust appears on the piece – this is called firescale. This can be removed using a pickle solution, but the aim is to prevent the firescale from forming on the fired metal in the first place. Follow these steps to ensure your pieces of bronze and copper clay are fully sintered with minimal firescale. The method for firing both metal clays by gas torch is exactly the same.

FIRING WITH A GAS TORCH

This method is best for pieces measuring no larger than 3cm x 3cm x 5mm (1¼ x 1¼ x ¼in). Pieces containing cubic zirconia, gemstones, glass or ceramics should not be fired with a gas torch.

1 Place the dried copper or bronze clay piece on the centre of a fire-resistant block.

2 Place a large heat-resistant container of cold water next to the firing block. Ignite the gas torch and direct the flame towards the metal clay piece at a 45-degree angle. Hold the torch at a distance of about 5cm (2in).

top tip

It is quite difficult to overheat or melt copper and bronze clay pieces because they need to reach continuous temperatures of 900°C (1652°F), for copper clay, and 820°C (1508°F) for bronze clay. Instead, your biggest concern is likely to be ensuring the pieces reach a hot enough temperature for a long enough time to become fully sintered.

3 Slowly move the flame over the piece to heat it evenly. You will see a little smoke and flame as the binder burns away. Concentrate the heat on the piece until it turns a bright orange-red colour. At this point you can start to time the firing. Turn the lights off in the room so that you can clearly see the colour of the hot metal. Continue to heat for the recommended length of time (according to the instructions on pages 138–139).

4 As soon as the firing is complete, quench the piece in cold water. Do not wait for the piece to cool because the moment the heat is no longer concentrated on the metal it will begin to oxidise. Quenching the heat immediately helps to prevent the piece from developing firescale.

5 You will need to pickle your pieces to remove any firescale – follow the instructions on page 31.

KILN FIRING GUIDE

A kiln allows you to fire large pieces with no restrictions on the weight of the copper or bronze clay. I have found that the following method is the safest and most effective way of kiln firing Art Clay copper and Prometheus copper and bronze clay.

1 Place the dried piece, or pieces, on a piece of stainless steel mesh on top of a gas stove. Fire for 10 minutes, then allow to cool down.

2 Put approximately 3cm (1¼in) of coconut-activated carbon in the bottom of a steel box.

3 Place your clay piece inside the box – if you are firing more than one piece, position them so that there is at least 1.5cm (½in) space between them. Cover the piece with coconut-activated carbon, then put the lid on.

4 Place the box in the preheated kiln: 820°C (1508°F) for Prometheus bronze clay and 900°C (1652°F) for Art Clay copper and Prometheus copper clay. Allow the kiln to reach the target temperature again and set your timer to fire for 60 minutes. When the firing is complete, either leave the pieces to cool down in the kiln or carefully take out the box and leave it on a heat-resistant surface until it is cool enough to remove the pieces.

top tip
You can fire a mix of copper and bronze pieces at the same time: heat the kiln to 820°C (1508°F) and fire for two hours.

PICKLING COPPER AND BRONZE CLAY

Pickling is the process of removing impurities from metal. Traditionally, a pickle solution used in jewellery making would contain hydrochloric or sulphuric acid. Today we now have access to what are known as 'safety pickles'. These contain fruit acids, so they are safe to use and not harmful to the skin. You will need to place your fired bronze and copper pieces in a warm pickle solution. The heat and the acid will erode any oxidisation from the piece. Some pieces take longer to pickle than others; this all depends upon the amount of firescale present on the piece.

1 In a slow cooker, or saucepan, add some pickle powder to cold water – follow the manufacturer's instructions for quantities. Place a lid on the cooker or saucepan and heat the solution until it is hot, but not boiling.

2 Place the metal into the solution using copper or plastic tongs and re-cover the pot. Leave the piece to pickle for between 5–30 minutes.

3 Lift the metal out of the pickle. If oxidation remains, return it to the pickle and check it every minute until it is clean.

top tip

Follow the manufacturer's instructions carefully for mixing the pickle solution – each type contains different ingredients and has its own safety precautions for safe disposal after use.

4 Rinse the piece in cold water.

5 Brush the piece with a wire brush to remove any remaining pickle and to reveal the metal.

31

Turning your metal clay into jewellery

Once you have made your beautiful metal clay creations, what will you do with them? The most exciting part of jewellery making is selecting different materials to showcase your designs in just the right way.

Materials

As well as the essentials that enable your creations to be worn, such as jump rings, chain and earring wires, here are some important materials to consider adding to your craft box to bring your designs to life.

GEMSTONES AND BEADS

I have used a variety of different gemstones in the projects within this book to string necklaces and bracelets or to add as embellishments to earrings. I like to combine genuine gemstones with my precious metal designs because they honour the beauty and rarity of the metal much more than plastic or faux beads. These days natural gemstones have become much more affordable, so adding a beautiful, high-quality element to your jewellery does not have to break the bank.

CHAINS

Sterling silver chain is the perfect partner for creations made from silver clay, while copper and bronze pieces look wonderful with vintage chain. It is important to choose the style of chain that fits best with your design – sometimes a plated or fashion chain with large or unusually shaped links will be

the best choice. It is often worth browsing around charity shops for old pieces of jewellery from which you can upcycle chain.

FINDINGS

To make the projects in this book, and any future projects, you will need to build up a collection of jewellery findings. These are the crucial components that enable you to turn your metal clay, chain and beads into jewellery. Findings include jump rings (small rings that connect components together), earring wires, clasps, head pins, eye pins, crimps and crimp covers. Consider whether you would like to use sterling silver or plated findings, or choose from a range of metal colours including, silver, copper, gold, rose gold and antique bronze.

THREADING MATERIALS

You will need beading thread (also known as tiger tail) for threading beads to form a necklace or bracelet. Different gauges of wire are also useful during jewellery making, for example for setting pearls on pages 48–57. You can also use wire to create bails on fired pieces and to attach other components or materials to your metal pieces.

OTHER MATERIALS

Glossy, vibrant perspex is highly decorative and can be used to complement your metal clay pieces, see pages 70–73. Resin is ideal for attaching crushed gemstones to metal clay after firing, see pages 102–105, and can also be used as a protective or colourful glaze, see pages 96–97.

   Leather and textiles are a wonderful way to add colour and interest to a metal clay piece. They can provide a perfect backdrop, so that the metal clay piece becomes the focal point or simply a beautiful accent, see pages 60–63.

Tools

These are the main tools you will need for jewellery making. They are essentials and I have used them in virtually every project in this book.

FLAT NOSE PLIERS

Flat nose pliers come in various sizes and are used to bend sharp corners in wire and for holding things flat, straightening wire and opening and closing jump rings.

ROUND NOSE PLIERS

Round nose pliers are used for making loops and coils in wire, head pins and eye pins.

CRIMPING PLIERS

Crimping pliers are used to press crimps together to seal the end of beading thread on necklaces and bracelets (see page 36).

SIDE CUTTERS

Side cutters are essential for cutting beading thread and wire and for trimming the excess wire from head pins, eye pins and rivets.

BEZELLING TOOLS

A bezel rocker and curved bunisher tools are used to set gemstones in bezel wire after firing.

HAMMERS

A raw hide mallet and small jeweller's hammer are useful tools to own. A raw hide mallet is used to flatten or to reshape pieces after firing; a jeweller's hammer is used for riveting and flattening wire.

TWEEZERS

Fine tweezers are useful for setting stones, picking up hot pieces and for other fine detail work.

RING-MAKING TOOLS

When you are making rings you will need a wooden ring mandrel to place your clay on as it dries. A ring gauge and ring sizing papers for measuring precise ring sizes are both very useful tools.

Basic jewellery techniques

HOW TO OPEN AND CLOSE JUMP RINGS

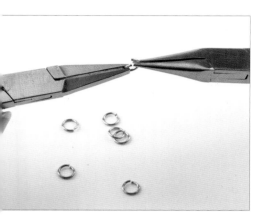

1 Use two pairs of pliers to grip the jump ring on either side of the gap. Move one side towards you and the other away from you to open the jump ring. Do not pull the ring apart because it may distort the shape.

2 Once you have opened the jump ring, you can insert an earring wire, chain, clasp or another jump ring.

3 To close the jump ring, grip both ends with your pliers. Bend them back together again, wiggling the ends back and forth until you feel them sliding against one another. Your jump ring ends should be perfectly aligned when it is closed correctly.

HOW TO WRAP A WIRE LOOP

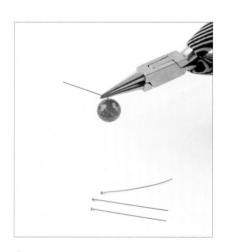

1 Thread a bead onto a head pin. Grip the head pin approximately 4mm (1/8in) above the bead with your round nose pliers. Bend the head pin to a right angle.

2 Use your free hand to bend the tail of the head pin around the top jaw of your pliers to form a complete loop. You might have to reposition your pliers to do this.

3 Grip the loop with your flat nose pliers. Use your free hand to wrap the wire around the neck of the loop until it touches the bead. Trim off the excess wire as close to the wrap as possible using your side cutters.

STRINGING A BEADED NECKLACE OR BRACELET

1 Thread the required number of beads onto a length of beading thread. Allow at least 10cm (4in) of excess thread at either end.

2 Thread a crimp onto one end of the beading thread.

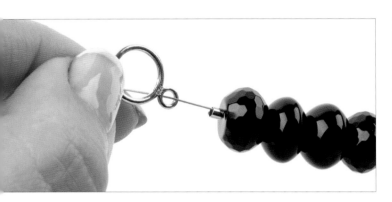

3 Next thread on the jump ring of the clasp.

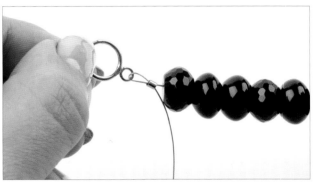

4 Take the beading thread back through the crimp and pull the thread tightly to tighten the loop of thread around the jump ring of the clasp.

5 Press the crimp together using crimping pliers or flat nose pliers.

6 Trim off the excess thread or push it through as many beads as possible then trim. Repeat this process at the other end of the necklace or bracelet.

MAKING A LOOP IN WIRE

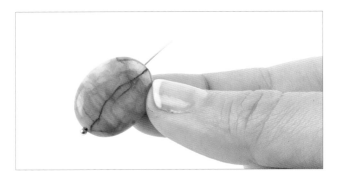

1 Thread a bead onto a head pin or eye pin.

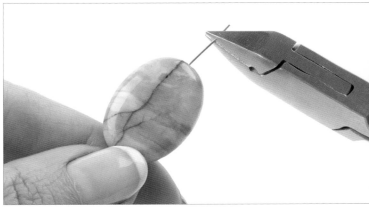

2 Trim the wire above the bead to about 1cm (½in).

3 Hold the end of the wire with round nose pliers and bend the wire over to form a semi-circle.

4 Let go of the wire, move the pliers around the loop a little, then continue to roll the wire until you have formed a circular loop centred above the bead.

5 Use your flat nose pliers to open the loop away from you as if you were opening a door.

6 Attach the loop to your finding or piece of jewellery then use your flat nose pliers to bend the loop in the opposite direction to close it.

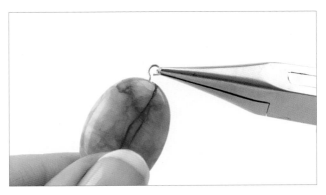

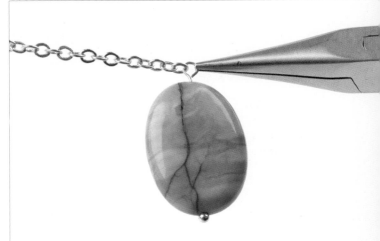

Creating texture

The biggest advantage that metal clays have over traditional sheet metal is that it is incredibly easy to add texture to them. No hammering or piercing is needed, nor the effort of putting the metal through a rolling mill – simply sculpt or roll out your clay and press the texture of your choice into it. The hardest task will be choosing which textures you want to use. Here are a few ideas and methods to inspire your creativity.

Using moulds

Pre-made moulds are widely available to buy, but making your own using two-part moulding putty is simple, fun and can be very effective. When mixed, the two parts 'cure', or set, to form a mould that you can use again and again. Moulding putty is usually silicone-based and therefore very flexible. It allows you to capture all the fine detail of your chosen object, so is ideal for moulding delicate, detailed items such as the shell, used here. Simply press your metal clay into the cured mould and allow to dry. After drying, finishing and firing, you are left with a beautiful piece of precious metal that is an exact replica of the item the mould was taken from.

1 Two-part silicone moulding putty is supplied in two separate containers, part A and part B. You will need an equal quantity of each.

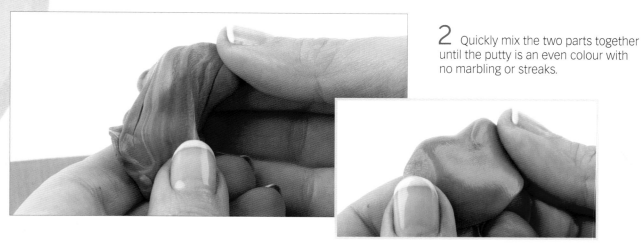

2 Quickly mix the two parts together until the putty is an even colour with no marbling or streaks.

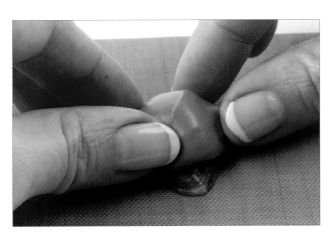

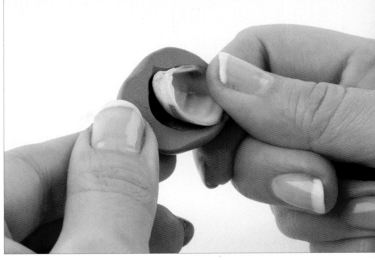

3 Press the mixed putty onto the object you would like to take a mould of. Distribute the putty so that it is an even thickness all over the object. Allow the putty to cure and set according to the manufacturer's instructions.

4 Press your nail into the edge of the mould to check if it has fully cured. If your nail leaves an impression in the silicone, the putty has not yet cured. Once the mould has cured, gently flex it to release the original object. The mould is flexible and the object should pop out quite easily. Be careful not to tear the mould.

5 To create a silver clay mould, mix the clay with a little water to soften it, and knead it in a piece of plastic wrap. If you are using copper or bronze clay, add a little liquid glycerine instead of water.

6 Push your clay into the mould. Press firmly and distribute the clay evenly. Remove any excess clay with your fingers or trim with a tissue blade. Press a texture onto the back of the mould if desired.

7 Allow the clay to dry inside the mould. Once dry, gently lift the edges of the mould to release your dry clay piece. Refine and finish your metal clay piece before firing it.

Using texture stamps

Adding texture to your clay creates a beautiful effect. The best textures to use are rubber texture mats specially designed for use with metal clays, although you can also use polymer clay textures, metal texture plates and plastic embossing sheets for paper crafts. It is worth experimenting with texture and improvising by using textured paper, lace, textiles and found objects such as tree bark, stones, shells, leaves – in fact anything with an interesting texture is worth a try: the results can be fabulous.

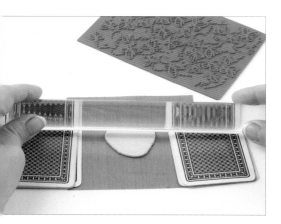

top tip

If you prefer to be more precise you can roll the texture onto your clay with a rolling pin. Roll the clay out to a thicker depth than required and remove one or two playing cards from both sides. Apply some clay balm to the texture sheet and place it on top of the clay so that it sits between the two stacks of cards. Press it into the clay by rolling over it.

1 Adding texture will make your clay thinner, so roll your clay out one or two playing cards thicker than the finished depth you want. Remove the playing cards. Add some clay balm to the texture sheet with a toothbrush.

2 Press all or part of the sheet onto the rolled clay. Press firmly to ensure that the texture creates a deep enough impression, but avoid squashing the clay too thinly.

3 Holding the texture sheet in place, lift the edge to check that you have achieved the desired effect. If not, press the texture sheet down again more firmly. If you have pressed too hard, gather up the clay, re-roll it and try again.

4 Always add texture to your metal clay before cutting out your shapes.

Making a polymer clay relief

Polymer clay is an excellent way to capture texture and it can be used as an alternative to moulding putty. Polymer clay needs to be baked in order for it to keep its shape, but after this the texture or shape you have captured can be used again and again.

1 Condition your polymer clay before use. Roll it out and knead it thoroughly or put it through a clay rolling machine until it is smooth and soft enough to work with.

2 Press your conditioned polymer clay onto the object or surface you would like to take an impression of.

3 Slowly peel away the polymer clay. If you are happy with the result, place it on a lined baking tray and bake according to the manufacturer's instructions. Trim it to size before baking if you want a specific shape.

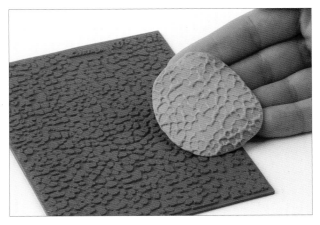

4 Once the polymer clay has been baked and is cool it is ready to use. Add some clay balm to the surface before rolling it onto metal clay or pressing metal clay onto it.

5 You can use polymer clay to take a reverse impression of rubber texture stamps. This will give you two different design options from one texture stamp.

Making a scratch foam relief

Scratch foam is a thin sheet of polystyrene that you can etch an image or pattern into. You can unleash your creative side and etch your designs freehand, or you could trace over an existing design. You can use your scratch foam relief directly on metal clay or you can take a mould of it with polymer clay or moulding putty.

TRACING YOUR DESIGN

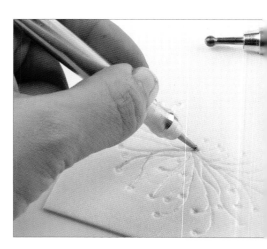

1 Cut a piece of scratch foam to the size you need for your design.

2 Tape your design to the foam. Trace over the design with a ballpoint pen. Press firmly so that you transfer the shapes onto the foam beneath.

3 Remove the paper design from the foam. Use an embossing stylus to enhance and deepen the etched lines.

CREATING IMPRESSIONS

You can use different sizes of embossing stylus to create deeper or wider impressions and grooves in the foam. This will give your relief a more three-dimensional look.

DRAWING FREEHAND

If you prefer, you can draw your design straight into the scratch foam. Use a ballpoint pen to create the initial design. Follow this with the embossing stylus to create the effects you would like.

IMPRINTING YOUR DESIGN

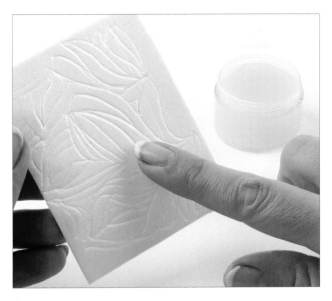

1 You can use the scratch foam relief directly on your metal clay. Add a light film of clay balm to the foam first.

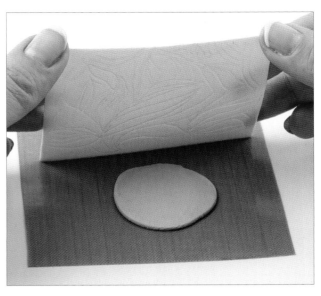

2 Roll out your metal clay to the desired thickness then place the scratch foam relief on top of it.

3 Use your rolling pin to roll the scratch foam texture into the clay.

4 Gently peel the scratch foam away to reveal the textured clay. Cut and shape your clay as desired. Clean the foam with a damp baby wipe to remove any excess clay.

Scratch Foam Earrings

These earrings are perfect for trying out your scratch foam designs. This project shows how quickly and simply your own unique textures can be brought to life. Consider what shape of earrings would work best with your chosen texture so that the whole design flows beautifully.

MATERIALS

Scratch foam with embossed design (see pages 42–43)

10g (¹⁄₃ oz) silver clay

Playing cards

Clay balm

Rolling pin

Triangle template

Tissue blade

Sponge sanding pad

Pin vice

Firing equipment

Wire brush

Agate burnisher

Metal polish and cloth

Flat nose pliers

Round nose pliers

Side cutters

2 silver fishhook earring wires

10cm (4in) silver chain

6 silver jump rings

2 silver head pins

2 black centre drilled drop beads, 12mm (½in)

1 Create a scratch foam relief according to the instructions on pages 42–43. Roll out your silver clay to a depth of six playing cards; if you want to make the design using bronze or copper clay, use seven playing cards.

2 Remove one of the playing cards on each side and place the scratch foam relief on top of your rolled clay. Use your rolling pin to roll across the scratch foam to press the texture into the clay.

3 Carefully peel the scratch foam away from the clay. Use a shape template to create your triangles – position it carefully then push it into the clay to mark your triangles.

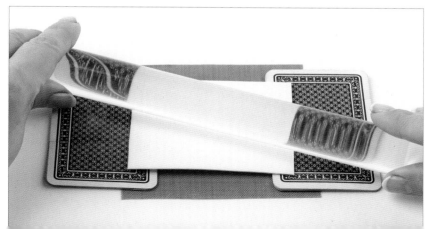

4 Use a tissue blade to cut out your earring shapes. Alternatively, you could use a cutter to create your shapes. You may need to re-roll and re-texture the clay to get your second earring shape and design perfect.

5 Set the clay aside to dry out thoroughly according to the instructions on pages 20–21. After the clay has dried, carefully smooth and refine any rough edges or imperfections with a sponge sanding pad.

6 Use a pin vice to drill holes in the dry clay, one in each corner of each triangle, for your jewellery findings to fit through after firing.

7 Fire your metal clay earrings according to the instructions on pages 138–139. Use a brass or wire brush to remove the white layer and reveal the silver.

top tip

If you have made your earrings from copper or bronze clay, you may need to place them in a hot pickle solution for 5–30 minutes to remove any firescale, before brushing them with a wire brush (see page 31).

8 Polish your earrings with an agate burnisher – this useful tool is ideal for giving a high shine to edges or areas with texture. Finish with metal polish to bring a high shine to the metal.

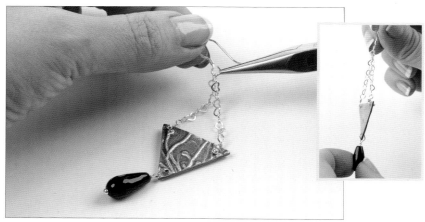

9 Thread silver head pins through the top two holes of one triangle, wrap these into loops and use them to attach lengths of silver chain and an earring hook (see page 35). Thread a bead with a silver head pin, then pass the wire through the bottom hole and wrap it neatly back around itself, following the instructions on page 35. Repeat for the other earring.

Alternative designs

You could use bronze, copper or silver clay to create stunning designs in other shapes. Make sure that both the shape of your earrings and the beads you attach complement the texture used.

Sea Urchin Necklace

I love to use shells and other objects from the sea because they have beautiful textures that look delightful captured in metal clay. I found the sea urchin shell that was used in this project in a little gift shop by the ocean on Coronado Island, San Diego. It was a wonderful trip and these pieces of jewellery will help to remind me of it forever.

MATERIALS

Small sea urchin shell
Two-part moulding putty
Snake roller
15g (½oz) copper clay
Plastic wrap
Sponge sanding pad
Pin vice with metal burr
Small spatula tool
Embeddable copper bail, 6mm (¼in) long
5cm (2in) copper wire, 0.8mm (¹⁄₁₆in) gauge
Firing equipment
Pickling equipment
Wire brush

Agate burnisher
Two-part resin
Half-drilled pearl: 6mm (¼in)
Awl
Flat nose pliers
Round nose pliers
Side cutters
80cm (32in) beading thread
46cm (18in) strand of light blue pearls, 8mm (¹⁄₆in) diameter
10 white pearls, 12mm (½in) diameter
2 copper-coloured crimps
2 copper-coloured crimp covers
Copper-coloured clasp

1 Take a mould of the sea urchin with two-part moulding putty, following the instructions on pages 38–39.

2 When the mould is in place, use a snake roller to flatten the top of it. This will leave the mould with a level base – if you ever want to pour resin or jewel enamel into it, a flat base will ensure that the mould keeps the contents level.

3 If need be, condition your copper clay using a few drops of liquid glycerine. Knead the clay in some plastic wrap until it is smooth and malleable (see page 19).

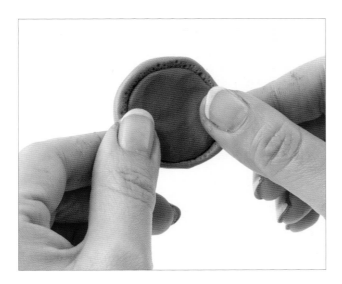

4 Roll the copper clay into a ball and press it into a round patty shape. Push the clay into the centre of the mould, making sure it is firmly and evenly inserted. Allow the clay to dry inside the mould in a warm place for 30 minutes.

5 Carefully remove the clay from the mould. Allow the clay to dry thoroughly according to the instructions on pages 20–21. Once the clay has dried, refine and sand the edges and the back. Do not sand the front of the piece, or you will remove the sea urchin shell texture.

6 Use a pin vice to drill a hole through the centre of the sea urchin pendant. Use a metal burr to hollow out the centre so that when the pearl is attached it will be slightly embedded in the surface. Then use a pin vice to drill a hole in the top of the pendant – this is where you will attach your copper bail.

7 Add a little water to some copper clay to make a sticky paste. Mix the paste using a small spatula tool.

8 Apply paste to the end of the embeddable copper bail. Push the bail through the hole at the top of the pendant. Use the paste to glue the bail in place, creating a thick layer on the back of the pendant.

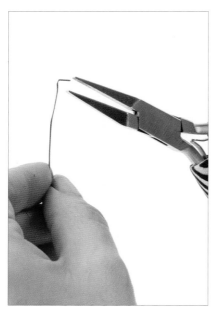

9 Take the 5cm (2in) length of copper wire and bend the end at a right angle to create a 5mm (¼in) foot.

10 Push the wire through the hole in the centre of the pendant, so that the foot is at the back. Cover the wire foot and seal it in place with copper paste.

11 Allow the clay to dry thoroughly before doing any final sanding and smoothing. Fire the pendant according to the instructions on pages 138–139. Place the pendant in a hot pickle solution for 5–30 minutes to remove any firescale.

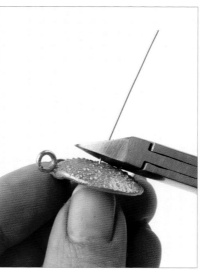

12 Brush the pendant to bring out the copper colour. Polish the front and edges with an agate burnisher.

13 Trim the copper wire, so that it is short enough to fit inside the pearl.

14 Mix some two-part resin glue and apply a little to the wire. Stick the pearl onto the wire and allow to dry for 24 hours before wearing.

Sea Urchin Ring

This gorgeous ring uses the same sea urchin mould as the previous project, but to very different effect. Pairing the textured silver clay with the smooth grey pearl creates a wonderful contrast and a striking piece of jewellery.

MATERIALS

Ring measuring gauge

Ring sizing papers

Scissors

Wooden ring mandrel

20g (¾oz) silver clay

Playing cards

Clay balm

Rolling pin

Tissue blade

Needle tool

Sponge sanding pad

Silver syringe clay

Paintbrush

Small sea urchin shell

Two-part moulding putty

Domed object, such as a door knob or small ball

Pin vice with metal burr

Circle cutter: the size of the base of your sea urchin mould

5cm (2in) fine silver wire, 0.8mm (¹/₁₆ in) gauge

Firing equipment

Wire brush

Metal polish and cloth

Two-part resin

Half drilled pearl: 6mm (¼in)

Flat nose and round nose pliers

Wire clippers

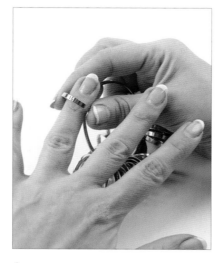

1 Measure your finger using a ring measuring gauge. You will be making a ring with a slim shank so you should add two sizes to the ring to allow for shrinkage. For example, if your ring size is 15, you need to make a ring that is size 17. The clay will shrink to a size 15 during drying and firing.

2 Take a ring sizing paper and cut off the excess paper at the cut mark – this is at the sticky end of the paper.

3 Wrap the ring sizing paper around a ring mandrel starting with the non-sticky edge. Adjust the paper until the sticky edge meets the correct measurement line on the paper. Stick the edge down firmly.

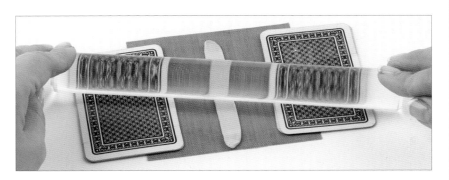

4 Take 10g (⅓oz) of silver clay and roll this into a strip that is long enough to wrap around the ring mandrel and overlap by about 2cm (¾in); roll your clay to a thickness of five playing cards.

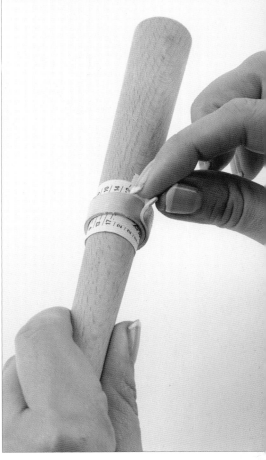

5 Trim the edges of the strip of clay with a tissue blade, so that you create a neat, straight-sided strip that is about 1cm (½in) wide.

6 Wrap the clay around the mandrel so that the ends overlap.

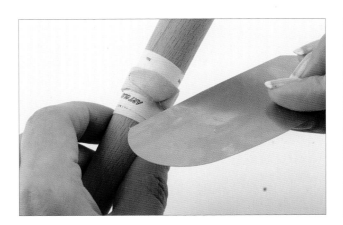

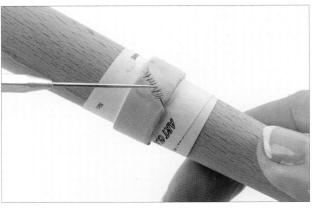

7 Cut through the overlap with a tissue blade at an angle of about 45 degrees; this will create a closer joint when you join the two ends together.

8 Use a needle tool or other sharp instrument to bind the two pieces of clay together. Make light, dovetail-style incisions to pull the two pieces of clay together – this method creates a smooth joint on the ring. Allow the ring to dry on the mandrel for about 30 minutes.

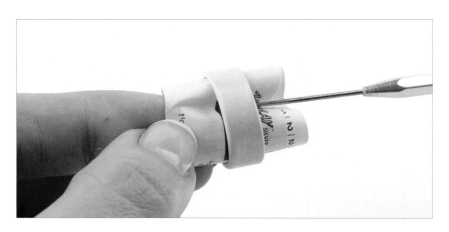

9 Slip the ring off the mandrel by gently twisting the ring sizing paper. Carefully insert a needle tool between the paper and the ring and push the paper inwards to remove it.

10 Smooth any rough areas around the edge, outside and inside of the ring with a sponge sanding pad. Add some syringe clay to fill the join inside and out. Smooth the join using a paintbrush. Allow the ring to dry again. Repeat the process until you have a perfect finish and can no longer see or feel the join.

11 Create a mould of the sea urchin shell, following the instructions on pages 38–39. Take 10g (¹/₃ oz) of silver clay and roll it into a ball then press the ball into a patty shape. Place the clay in the centre of the sea urchin mould and push it firmly to distribute the clay evenly around the mould.

12 Gently peel the clay away from the mould taking care not to disturb the impression. Place the clay on top of a small domed object and form the clay over it. Allow the clay to dry on top of the object for 30 minutes.

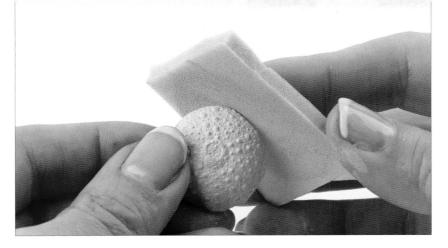

13 Remove the clay and allow it to dry thoroughly according to the instructions on pages 20–21. Once the clay is dry, sand and smooth it so that the edges are smooth.

14 Use a pin vice to drill a hole right through the centre of the clay shape.

15 Use a metal burr to hollow out the centre so that when the pearl is attached it will be slightly embedded within the pendant.

16 Take the 5cm (2in) length of silver wire and bend the end at a right angle to create a 5mm (¼in) foot. Push the wire through the hole in the centre of the pendant, so that the foot is at the back. Add some syringe or paste clay to seal the hole and cover the foot.

17 Roll out a circle of silver clay, three playing cards thick, and cut a small circle from it, using your cutter.

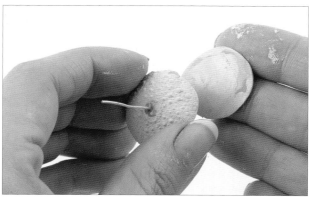

18 Wet the circle of clay and place the sea urchin piece on top of it. Stick the two pieces together firmly, then use a wet paintbrush to help blend the edges of the two pieces of clay together. Allow to dry completely.

19 Do any final sanding and smoothing of the domed shape. Apply a generous amount of syringe clay to the ring and stick it onto the back of the sea urchin shape. Use a wet paintbrush to remove any excess clay. Allow the whole piece to dry (see pages 20–21).

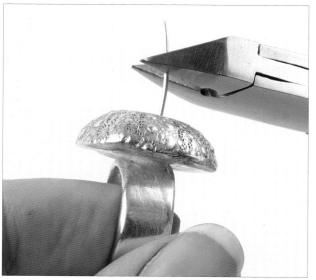

20 Fire the ring according to the instructions on pages 138–139. After firing, brush and polish the entire ring. Trim the wire so that it is short enough to fit inside the pearl.

21 Mix some two-part resin glue and apply a little to the wire. Stick the pearl onto the wire and allow to dry for 24 hours before wearing.

Creating bas reliefs

Bas relief is a sculptural technique in which a three-dimensional design is raised above its background. This technique is achieved in sculpture by chiselling away at the background to create an object that stands out in relief; with metal clays we can layer the design on top of the background to create the same three-dimensional effect much more easily.

Creating a bas relief

The secret to creating an authentic looking bas relief effect in metal clay is to smooth the object in the foreground into the background, rather than just sticking the two pieces of clay together. Create your background first and allow the clay to dry fully before adding the relief effect. It is important to join the top piece while it is still wet clay to the dry base clay. The careful sealing of the top and bottom layers helps to join the two pieces of clay together very securely. This is especially important when connecting two pieces of copper or bronze clay because they don't fuse in the same way that silver clay does.

1 Roll and cut out a piece of metal clay to use as your background. This will be the main supporting piece of your design: if you are using silver clay, roll it to a thickness of five playing cards. If you are using copper or bronze clay, roll it to a thickness of six playing cards. Refer to pages 16–19 for further information. Here, copper clay has been used – condition it first if need be (see page 19).

2 Allow the clay to dry out completely. Sand and smooth the edges, front and back of the base piece with a sponge sanding pad.

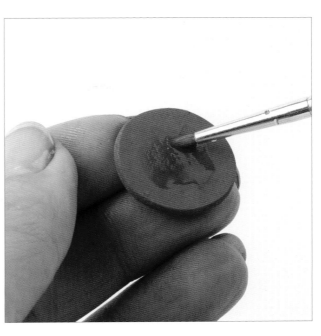

3 Roll and cut out the clay for the relief part of your design. If you are working with silver clay, roll out your clay to a thickness of two playing cards; if you are working with copper or bronze clay, roll out your clay to a thickness of three playing cards.

4 Use a small paintbrush to wet the dry base clay in the area where you would like to stick your clay shape.

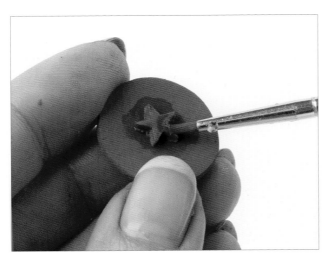

5 Place the piece of wet clay onto the base. Use a damp – not wet – paintbrush or a clay shaper to gently press the edges of the wet piece of clay into the dry base and blend and seal the two pieces together.

6 Keep blending slowly and carefully until the two pieces are seamlessly joined together. Continue to add any further pieces to your design in the same way. Allow the clay to dry fully before refining and smoothing any imperfections or rough areas.

Snake Bracelet

I was inspired by an ancient stone carving for this snake design. The curves of the snake contrast beautifully with the angles of the background. This would also look good made as a matching necklace.

MATERIALS

20g (¾oz) silver clay
Clay balm
Tissue blade
Ruler
Playing cards
Sponge sanding pad
Fish scale texture sheet
Small paintbrush
Snake roller
Clay shaper
Baby wipes
Silver paste clay
Pin vice
Needle file

Firing equipment
Wire brush
Metal polish and cloth
Agate burnisher
Flat nose pliers
Round nose pliers
Side cutters
Leather cuff
10cm (4in) silver wire (0.6mm gauge)
Leather glue
Small piece of soft leather, 20 x 10cm (8 x 4in)
Fabric scissors
Awl

1 Take 10g (⅓oz) of silver clay and roll it to a thickness of five playing cards. Use a tissue blade or craft knife to cut a rectangle of clay measuring 2.5 x 3cm (1 x 1¼in). This will form the base of your design.

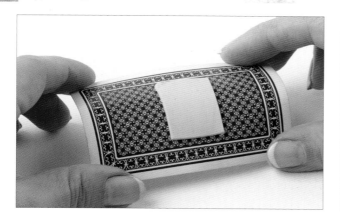

2 Place the piece of clay on top of a curved playing card and allow to dry according to the instructions on pages 20–21. When the clay is completely dry, sand and smooth any rough edges with a sponge sanding pad.

3 Take 10g (⅓oz) of silver clay and roll it to a thickness of two playing cards. Apply a thin layer of clay balm to your fish scale texture and press it into the clay. Cut a thin strip measuring 5mm (¼in) wide and about 4cm (1½in) long.

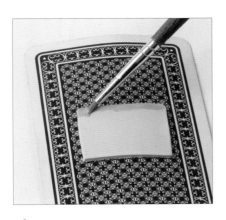
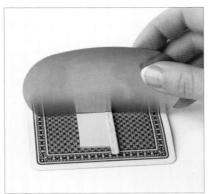

4 Wet one long edge of the dry clay base with a small paintbrush. Place the strip of wet clay along the edge of the dry clay base.

5 Trim off the excess clay at each end with a tissue blade or craft knife.

6 Cut the clay at a diagonal angle at each end to create the appearance of a mitred edge. Repeat this process along all four edges of the dry clay base. Set the base aside to dry.

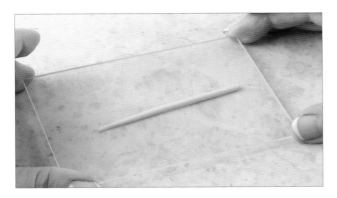
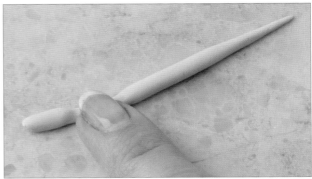

7 Take the excess clay and use a snake roller to roll a rope of clay about 5cm (2in) long. Use your fingers to roll one end of the clay to a point.

8 Form the other end of the rope of clay into a head by rolling your finger about 1cm (½in) from the end to create a slightly thinner 'neck'. Wet the rope of clay and allow it to become saturated with water for a few seconds.

9 Wet the central area of the clay base with a paintbrush. Using a wet paintbrush, coil the rope into a snake-like wiggle within the central area.

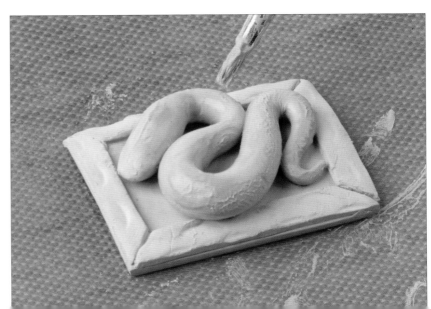

10 Use a damp paintbrush or a clay shaper to blend the bottom of the snake to the clay base.

11 Add some watery paste to the bottom of the snake to seal the join between it and the base. Keep smoothing until the two pieces are seamlessly connected.

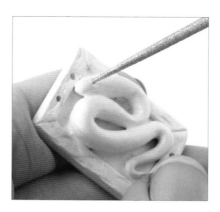

12 Allow the piece to dry according to the instructions on pages 20–21. After drying, sand and smooth the piece using a damp baby wipe and a sponge sanding pad. Drill two holes through each side of the silver base using a pin vice.

13 Use a needle file to drill an eye or eyes into the head of the snake.

14 Fire the piece according to the instructions on pages 138–139. After firing, allow the piece to cool or quench it in cold water. Brush the pendant with a wire brush to reveal the silver. Polish the piece and use an agate burnisher to polish the edges.

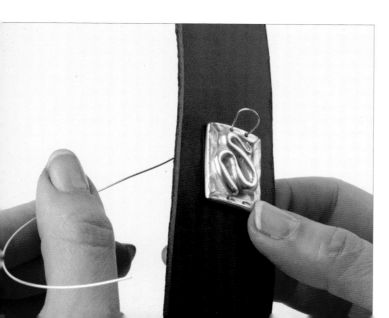

15 It is easiest to attach the pendant to a pre-bought leather cuff, although you can create your own if you want. Position the pendant where you want it on the cuff, then push an awl through the pendant's holes to mark pilot holes on the cuff. Make holes in the leather cuff using the awl. Thread silver wire through the pendant and cuff holes and twist the ends off to secure, hiding any sharp ends. Stick another piece of soft leather onto the back of the cuff with leather glue to cover the wire. Alternatively, you could attach the silver pendant to some beads to create a more delicate bracelet.

Lovebirds Pendant

This sweet little pendant is another example of the effectiveness of using bas relief in a design, this time on bronze clay. This is a relatively small piece, so you may find using a magnifier helpful when cutting out and attaching the shapes.

MATERIALS

15g (½oz) bronze clay

Circle cutter: 3.5cm (1½in)

Domed object, such as a door knob or small ball

Clay balm

Rolling pin

Playing cards

Sponge sanding pad

Needle tool or craft knife

Small paintbrush

Tissue blade

Drinking straw

Pin vice

Needle file

Firing equipment

Pickling equipment

Wire brush

Flat nose pliers

Round nose pliers

Side cutters

9 bronze-coloured head pins

10 pearl beads, 6mm (¼in) diameter

1m (3½ft) bronze-coloured chain

2 bronze-coloured jump rings, 6mm (¾in)

Bronze-coloured lobster claw clasp

4cm (1½in) gold or bronze-coloured wire (0.6mm gauge)

1 To make the base of your pendant, roll out your bronze clay to a thickness of six playing cards. Cut out a circle shape with your cutter.

2 Place your circle of clay on top of a domed object to dry. Add some clay balm to the object first to prevent the clay from sticking. After drying, sand and smooth the clay to remove any imperfections or rough areas.

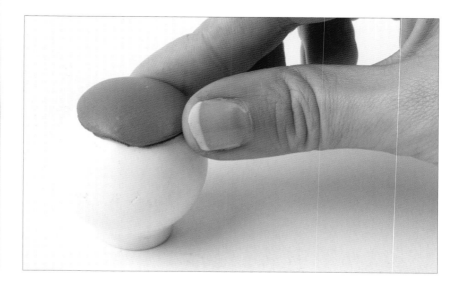

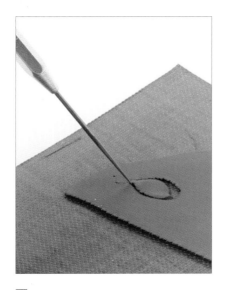  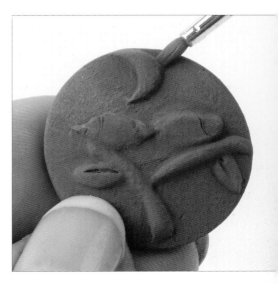

3 Roll out the excess bronze clay to a thickness of three playing cards. Cut out two bird shapes with a needle tool or craft knife. When cut, bronze clay shapes can become a little jagged, so smooth the edges of the birds with your fingers.

4 Add some watery paste to the back of each bird and also to the base of the pendant. Press the birds down gently onto the pendant base and begin to smooth the edges with a damp paintbrush or clay shaper. Do this until the birds have seamlessly joined the base.

5 Roll out a piece of bronze clay into a thin rope. Cut the rope into two and shape the ends to a point. Attach the two ropes of clay to the base with some watery bronze paste. They should sit under the birds to form the tree branches. Smooth the edges of the branches to create a seamless join. Cut out two leaf shapes and a crescent moon shape from the excess bronze clay and attach these to the pendant in the same way. Set the piece aside to dry.

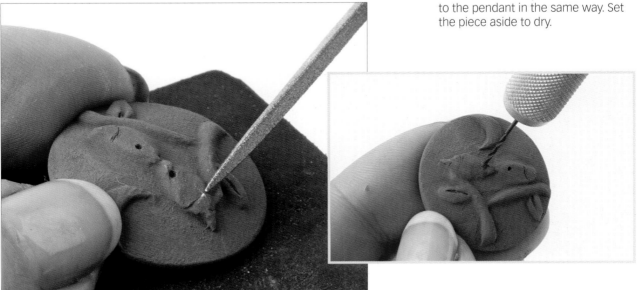

6 Add some definition to your shapes using a needle file and pin vice. Use the file to accentuate lines on the birds' wings and on the leaves, and use the pin vice to create eyes.

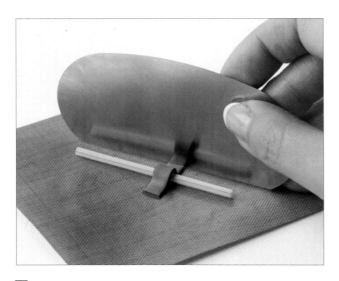

7 Roll out a 1.5cm (½in) long strip of bronze clay four playing cards thick and 5mm (¼in) wide to form the bail. Cut it to shape and place it over a drinking straw to dry.

8 When the bail and pendant are both completely dry, make a sticky paste by adding some water to some bronze lump clay and add this to the back of the bail. Attach the bail to the back of the pendant. Use a wet paintbrush to remove any excess clay and seal the join between the two pieces. Allow to dry.

9 Once the piece is completely dry, drill a small hole through the base of the pendant with a pin vice. Fire the pendant following the instructions on pages 138–139. After firing, place the pendant in a hot pickle solution to remove any firescale.

10 Brush the pendant with a wire brush to reveal the bronze metal.

11 Thread one of the pearls onto a head pin. Attach the head pin to the hole at the base of the pendant and form a wrapped loop according to the instructions on page 35. Thread some bronze-coloured chain through the bail. Thread a head pin onto each of the remaining pearls and attach these to the chain. Trim the chain to the required length and attach jump rings and a lobster claw clasp.

Making connections after firing

You might think that creating metal clay jewellery on a grand scale would be out of the question: precious metal clays, particularly silver clay, can be an expensive product to use and there is also a limit to the size of piece you can fire. But with a bit of creative design work it's possible to connect fired metal pieces not only to each other, but also to materials such as perspex, leather, glass, wood or polymer clay. In this section we will explore ways in which you can connect pieces together to give your design greater volume and add colour and interest.

Drilling holes

It is always easiest to make holes in your piece of metal clay before firing it. However, if you decide after firing that you would like to attach the piece to another object, or you have drilled holes that are not the right size, this is what you should do.

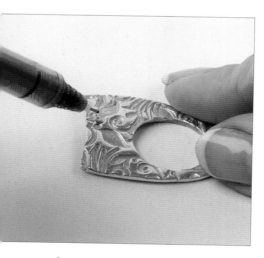

1 Mark the fired metal clay piece with a pen, in the position where you would like to drill the hole.

2 Use the end of a needle file to create a small pilot hole in the position of your pen mark.

3 Work out how large you want your hole to be, then attach the correctly sized drill bit to a rotary tool. Holding the drill upright and steady, drill through the metal, using your pilot hole as a guide. If you are using rivets, your drill bit needs to be exactly the same width as the rivet.

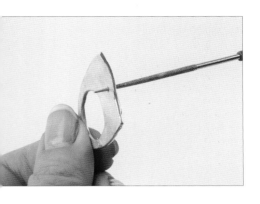

4 Use a needle file to finish the inside of the hole or to make it slightly larger if need be. If you need to make the hole significantly larger, change to a larger drill bit.

what next...

At this point you could simply attach the drilled piece onto a chain or other piece of jewellery using a jump ring. If you want to rivet it to another material, drill a hole of the same size on the object that you are connecting your metal clay piece to.

Using rivets

Rivets are available in different sizes and metal finishes. Sometimes the rivet's only function is to connect two components together as securely and discreetly as possible; on other occasions the rivet can become a feature of your design.

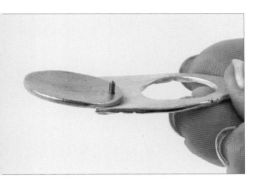

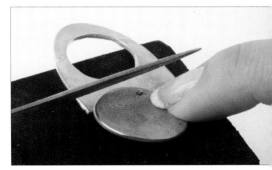

1 Check that your rivet will pass through the hole in both pieces. It needs to be a snug fit and should not be loose. If the hole is too small, carefully re-drill it to make it slightly larger; if the hole is too big you will need to select a thicker rivet. Slide the rivet through both components.

2 Cut the rivet to about 2mm (¹/₁₆ in) long. Use two playing cards to help measure the correct length.

3 Use a file to sand away the sharp point created by the wire cutters.

4 Lay your pieces on a hard surface, preferably a rubber block, with the protruding rivet end pointing upwards. Using a ball peen or chasing hammer, tap the rivet lightly and at an angle. Hit the rivet end so it spreads out slightly over the hole and creates a mushroom-like shape. Gradually increase the intensity of the hammer taps until both pieces are securely held together.

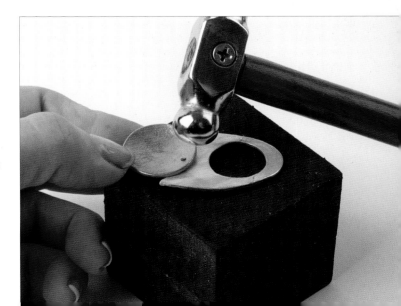

Copper Set On Perspex Pendant

I love using perspex in my designs because it is very cost effective and available in so many different colours and finishes. It is such a versatile material and is easy to cut and shape. The cobalt blue perspex works beautifully in contrast with the salmon pink colour of the copper clay accent here. Selecting different colours and finishes and cutting different shapes of perspex will make your designs look dramatically different every time.

MATERIALS

15g (½oz) copper clay

Playing cards

Rolling pin

Clay balm

Leopard print texture sheet

Templates (see page 143), card and scissors

Needle tool or craft knife

Sponge sanding pad

Pin vice

Firing equipment

Pickling equipment

Wire brush

Sheet of perspex – cobalt blue

Non-permanent pen

Jeweller's saw

Half-round metal file, 15cm (6in) long

3 copper nail head rivets – 6mm (¼in) long, 1.6mm (¹/₁₆in) thick

Masking tape

Rotary tool with 1.6mm (¹/₁₆in) drill bit

Ball peen or chasing hammer

1m (3½ft) leather cord, 1mm (¹/₆in) thick

1 To start, draw the metal clay and perspex templates on a piece of card and cut them out (see page 143). Roll out a piece of copper clay to a thickness of six playing cards. Apply a thin layer of clay balm to the leopard print texture mat. Press this firmly into the clay.

2 Place the template on the copper clay and cut around it using a needle tool or craft knife. Allow the clay to dry according to the instructions on pages 20–21.

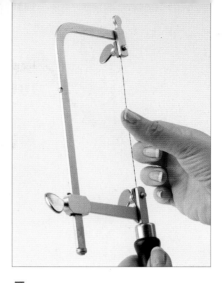

3 Sand and smooth the piece using a sponge sanding pad. With a pin vice, drill three pilot holes into the dry clay where you will insert your rivets. Fire according to the instructions on pages 138–139. Place the fired piece in a hot pickle solution for 5–30 minutes to remove the firescale.

4 Leave the protective covering on the perspex to prevent it from getting marked or scratched. Place the perspex template on top and draw around it using a non-permanent pen.

5 Attach a saw blade to the jeweller's saw frame. Ensure that the rough side of the blade is facing outwards with the teeth of the blade pointing downwards so that it feels rough against your skin when you run your finger up the blade.

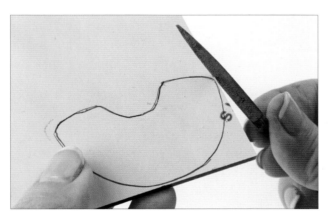
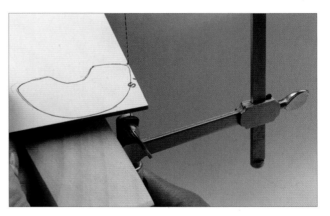

6 Make a groove in the perspex with a metal file where you want to begin cutting. Choose a point where the line comes close to the edge; a corner, as shown here, is ideal.

7 Move the saw up and down cutting along the line of the template you have drawn. Keep the saw as straight and vertical as you can while you cut through the perspex.

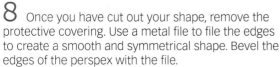

8 Once you have cut out your shape, remove the protective covering. Use a metal file to file the edges to create a smooth and symmetrical shape. Bevel the edges of the perspex with the file.

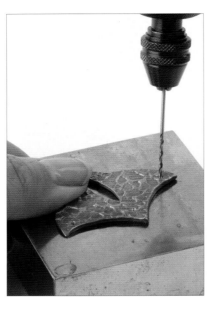

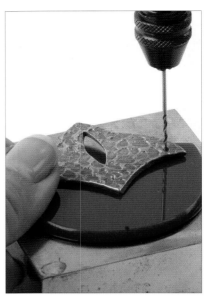

9 Use a sponge sanding pad to smooth and polish the edges.

10 Attach a 1.6cm (1/16in) drill bit to the rotary tool and drill the three holes in the copper pendant.

11 Place the perspex shape underneath the copper and stick the two pieces together with some masking tape. Drill through the holes in the copper pendant to create the corresponding holes in the perspex.

12 Remove the masking tape then slide a rivet through one set of holes in the copper and perspex. Attach the rivet according to the instructions on page 69. Repeat the process to attach all three rivets. Either attach the pendant to some simple leather cord, as shown, or create a wire loop and attach it to a chain or beaded wire.

Alternative designs

Combining black, sparkly perspex with a silver clay accent and a silver and pearl beaded chain creates a much more delicate piece with a very different feel.

Ring with Interchangeable Heads

This versatile ring is the perfect addition to any jewellery collection. It is made with silver clay and has a bolt screw embedded in it; a second piece of silver clay contains the corresponding nut. Simply slide different attachments onto the ring shaft and secure them in place with a silver clay-topped nut. You will have a great choice of different ring designs, using just one silver ring base. Why not create a different ring topper for every day of the week?

MATERIALS

Ring measuring gauge

Ring sizing papers

Wooden ring mandrel

14g (½oz) silver clay

Playing cards

Clay balm

Rolling pin

Tissue blade

Needle tool

Sponge sanding pad

Silver syringe clay

Bolt: 1cm x 8mm (½ x ³/₈in) and corresponding nut

Small paintbrush

Circle cutter: 1.5cm (½in)

Small domed object

Tweezers

Clay shaper

Firing equipment

Wire brush

Silver polish and cloth

For the ring toppers:
  Polymer clay
  Textured bronze clay

1 Measure your finger using a ring measuring gauge. You will be making a ring with a medium shank so you should add three sizes to the ring to allow for shrinkage during drying and firing. For example, if your ring size is 15, you will need to make a size 18 ring. Slide the gauge onto your mandrel to work out where you need to wrap your silver clay and mark the point with your finger.

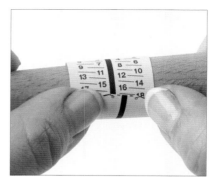

2 Wrap a ring sizing paper around the mandrel, starting with the non-sticky edge, so that the black line aligns with the point you marked with your finger. Adjust the paper until the sticky edge meets the correct measurement line. Stick down firmly.

3 Take 10g (¹/₃oz) of silver clay and roll this into a strip that is five playing cards thick and long enough to wrap around the ring mandrel and overlap by about 2cm (¾in).

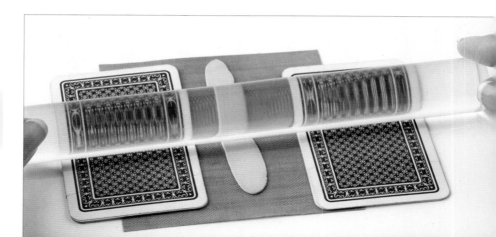

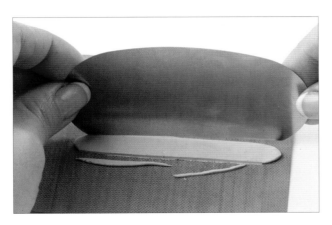

4 Trim the edges of the strip of clay so that the strip measures just under 1cm (½in) wide.

5 Wrap the clay around the mandrel so that the ends overlap. Cut through the overlap with a tissue blade at a slight angle – this will create a closer joint. Remove the two excess pieces of clay.

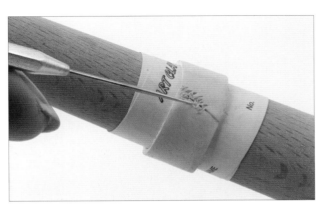

6 Use a needle tool or other sharp instrument to join the ends of the clay together. Make light, dovetail-style incisions to bind the clay together. This method creates a smooth joint on the ring. Allow the ring to dry on the mandrel for about 30 minutes.

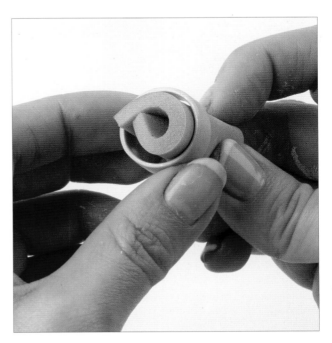

7 Slip the ring off the mandrel by gently twisting off the ring sizing paper. Carefully insert a needle tool between the paper and the ring and gently crumple the paper inwards to remove it from the clay ring. Smooth any rough areas around the edge, outside and inside the ring. Add some syringe clay to fill the join inside and outside the ring. Allow the ring to dry again. Repeat the process until you have a perfect finish and can no longer see or feel the join.

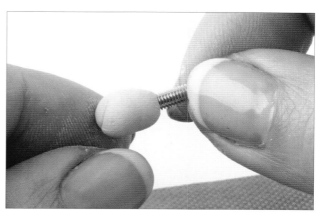

8 Take a small piece of silver clay and add a little water to make it softer. Roll it into a ball shape. Push the head of the bolt into the centre of the wet clay.

9 Sculpt and smooth the clay around the base of the bolt.

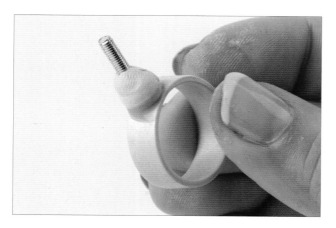

10 Attach this to the ring using some syringe clay.

11 Use your fingers and a wet paintbrush to smooth the clay all the way around the bolt and connect it to the ring shank. Allow the clay to dry.

12 Roll the remaining silver clay to a thickness of five playing cards. Use your cutter to cut out a circle shape. Place this on top of a small domed object such as a small ball. Smooth the edges down to create a smooth shape. Allow to dry for 20 minutes then remove the object and allow to dry out completely.

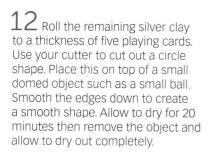

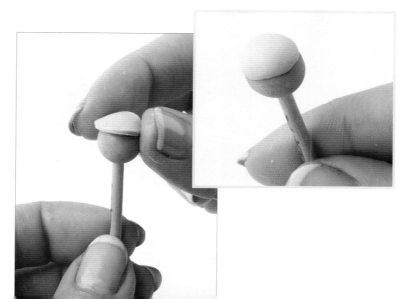

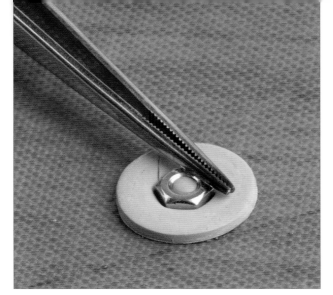

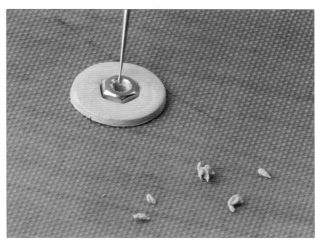

13 Roll out the remaining clay to a thickness of four playing cards. Cut out another circle shape. Push the nut into the centre of the clay using tweezers.

14 Remove the clay from the centre of the nut using a needle tool or other sharp, pointed tool.

15 Using a small paintbrush, brush around the edges of the clay circle with silver paste clay.

16 Place the domed piece of dry silver clay on top of the circle of clay. Smudge up the edges of the lower clay circle to seal the two pieces together. Use a clay shaper or wet paintbrush to seal the join between the two pieces. Allow to dry thoroughly.

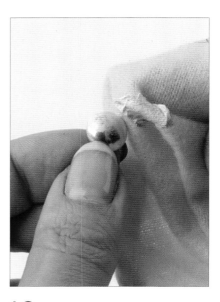

17 Sand and smooth both the ring and the dome-covered nut with a sponge sanding pad.

18 Fire the ring and nut according to the instructions on pages 138–139. After firing, cool the pieces and brush with a wire brush to reveal the silver.

19 Use silver polish and a cloth to make the ring and the nut shine.

20 Make some pieces to go on top of the ring: you can create shapes from metal or polymer clay or you could cut pieces of leather or perspex to use as toppers. Simply drill a hole in the centre of your creation and place it on the bolt shaft. Screw on the silver domed shape that contains the nut to hold the topper in place.

Working with coils

A wonderful property of metal clays is that you can roll them into ropes of any thickness or length. You can then coil these ropes to create wonderfully decorative effects, or coil them around another metal clay piece to create a frame or bezel. When I first began working with metal clays I struggled with making coils. Rolling the rope of clay was relatively easy, but I found that as soon as I began to bend the clay into the shape I wanted it would become dry and break. In this section I will share the techniques that now work for me every time, to help create smooth coils of clay that will enhance your metal clay designs.

Rolling a rope of clay

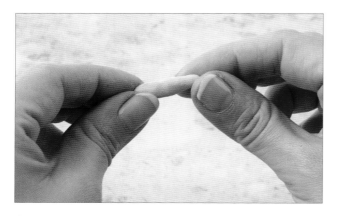

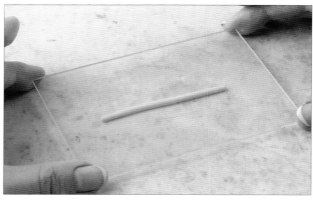

1 Pinch off a small piece of metal clay. Rolling the clay into a rope stretches it out, so you will use a lot less clay than when you are rolling it flat to cut out shapes. Roll the clay into a sausage shape with your fingers.

2 Place the clay on a flat, clean work surface – a smooth tile is ideal. You do not need to add any clay balm to the surface. Hold all four corners of the perspex sheet and place this on top of your clay.

3 Begin to the roll the perspex sheet back and forth across the clay quite vigorously. The more you roll the longer the rope of clay will become. If one end of the rope is thicker than the other, adjust the pressure you are placing on the perspex at that end of the clay to correct this. Once you have reached the desired lenth, use your finger to roll the ends into points.

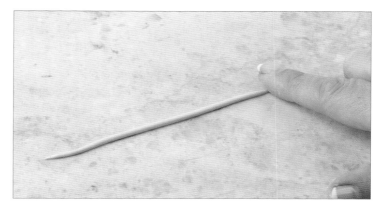

Forming coils

To form a smooth coil the clay needs to be well hydrated. As soon as you begin rolling the clay into a rope it begins to dry. This process happens much quicker than when you are rolling the clay out flat.

1 To create a coil that you will dry first before adding to your metal clay design, draw out the shape of the coil on a piece of greaseproof paper.

2 Roll a rope of clay following the instructions on the facing page. Dip your finger into a cup of water and run your wet finger along the length of the rope of clay. You need to saturate the clay – don't worry about getting it too wet. If the rope of clay does not look shiny and smooth, repeat the process and add more water. Allow the rope of clay to rehydrate for about 30 seconds.

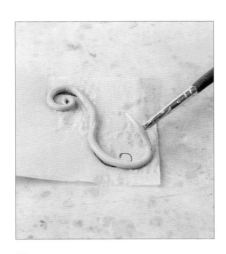

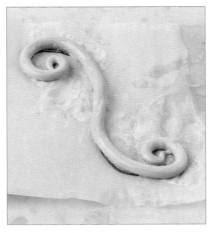

3 Pick up the rope of clay with a damp paintbrush and place it on the greaseproof paper. Use the paintbrush to carefully form it into the desired shape.

4 Allow the coil to dry. Carefully remove any rough areas using a dry paintbrush or a damp baby wipe. Attach the coil to your metal clay design with some paste clay.

top tip

If you are adding your coiled shape straight onto another piece of metal clay, pick up the rope with a small paintbrush. Place the rope onto your clay piece and use the paintbrush to form the rope into the shape you would like. Brush around the edges of the coil with some watery paste to seal it to your metal clay. Dry thoroughly before firing.

Mermaid Pendant

In this project I want to show how ropes of clay can be formed into gentle coils to create the sweeping curls of the mermaid's hair. The coils are also used to decorate her tail fin to make it look webbed and three-dimensional.

WHAT YOU NEED

30g (1oz) silver clay
Rolling pin
Clay balm
Playing cards
Templates (page 143), card and scissors
Needle tool
Fish scale texture sheet
Snake roller
Small paintbrush
Tissue blade
Drinking straw
Sponge sanding pad
Silver syringe clay
Pin vice
Fibre blanket
Firing equipment
Wire brushes
2 pairs of flat nose pliers
80cm (32in) silver chain
3 silver jump rings
Silver clasp

1 Create a template for the mermaid's head, body, tail and fin from a piece of card. Roll out a 20g (¾oz) piece of silver clay to a thickness of five playing cards. Place the mermaid body template onto the clay and cut around it using a needle tool or craft knife. Set the clay aside to dry.

2 Roll out a piece of silver clay six playing cards thick. Press the fish scale texture firmly onto the clay.

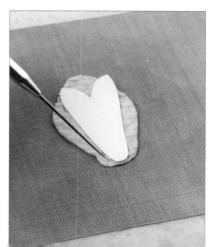

3 Remove the texture and place the large mermaid tail template onto the clay. Cut around it using a needle tool or craft knife. Set this aside to dry.

4 Roll out the remaining clay to a thickness of five playing cards. Place the fin template and head onto the clay and cut around them using a needle tool or craft knife. Set all the pieces aside to dry.

5 Take a small piece of clay and create a sausage shape. Use the snake roller to roll a long rope of clay.

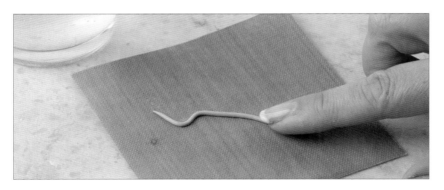

6 Saturate the clay with water using a wet paintbrush or your finger.

7 Allow the water to hydrate the clay for 30 seconds. Use your paintbrush to form the rope of clay into a long, sweeping curl of hair. Repeat this process eleven times to create twelve strands of hair. Allow the coils to dry.

8 Pinch off a small piece of silver clay and roll it into sausage to form an arm. Flatten the end of the shape to create a hand and bed this up slightly. Repeat the process to create the second arm and allow to dry.

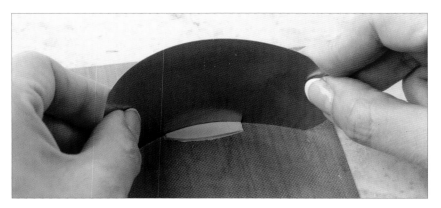

9 Roll a small piece of clay three playing cards thick and cut it into a strip about 2cm (¾in) long and 5mm (¼in) wide. Trim the edges of the clay to create a slightly rounded shape.

10 Wrap the shape over a length of drinking straw to create a bail.

11 Sand smooth all the pieces of the mermaid's body and tail using a sponge sanding pad.

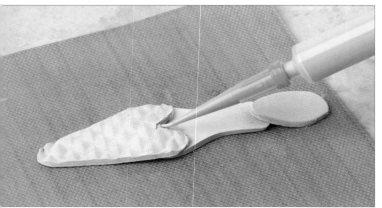

12 Use some silver syringe clay to stick the main tail piece and head to the body shape.

13 Use a wet paintbrush to remove any excess syringe clay and to seal the joins between the pieces.

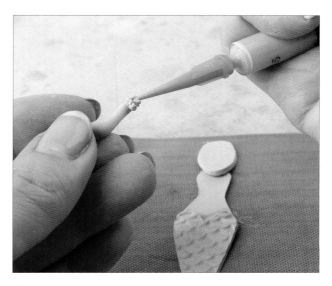

14 Attach the mermaid's arms by applying a generous amount of silver syringe clay to the top end, sticking it to the back of the mermaid's body so that the hands sit about level with the top of the tail and poke outwards. Use more syringe clay and a paintbrush to smooth over the join. Set aside to dry.

15 Attach the curls of hair to the mermaid's head using some syringe clay – you might want to work out how best they fit together before you start to attach them. Use a wet paintbrush to seal the pieces together. Allow to dry.

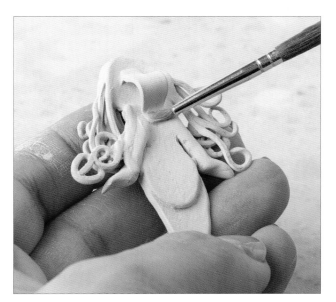

16 Attach the bail to the back of the mermaid using syringe clay and a damp paintbrush. Seal all the joins then allow the entire mermaid to dry completely.

17 Roll some thin ropes of clay and stick these to the tail fin using watery silver paste to give it a webbed appearance. Allow this to dry.

18 Sand and smooth the mermaid and her tail to remove any imperfections. Use a pin vice to drill a small hole in the bottom of the tail and top of the fin.

19 Fire the mermaid and fin according to the instructions on pages 138–139. Use fibre blanket to support the mermaid during firing, otherwise she will warp.

20 Brush the mermaid and fin to reveal the silver.

21 Use a smaller wire brush to polish the more intricate areas, such as within the coils of her hair.

22 Attach the fin to the tail section with a silver jump ring. You could thread the pendant onto a beaded necklace or cord; here a simple silver chain has been used.

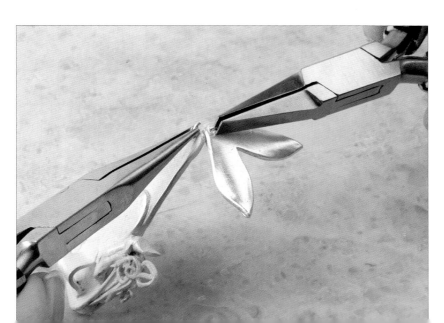

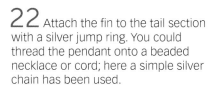

Italian-style Pendant

This design illustrates how coils of clay can fit together to form an overall design rather than being an addition to it. You can use the templates given to create a replica of this design, or create your own version by drawing simple shapes and seeing how they fit together. This piece can also be created using copper or bronze clay — simply mix a sticky paste from the lump clay to connect the coils together.

MATERIALS

Templates (page 143)
Greaseproof paper
10g (⅓oz) silver clay
Snake roller
Small paintbrush
Sponge sanding pad
Silver syringe clay
Firing equipment
Wire brush
Agate burnisher
Flat nose pliers
Round nose pliers
Side cutters
80cm (32in) beading thread
46cm (18in) strand of light
  blue quartz beads, 10mm
  (½in) diameter
12 light blue quartz beads,
  6mm (¼in) diameter
1 head pin
2 silver crimps
2 silver crimp covers
Silver clasp

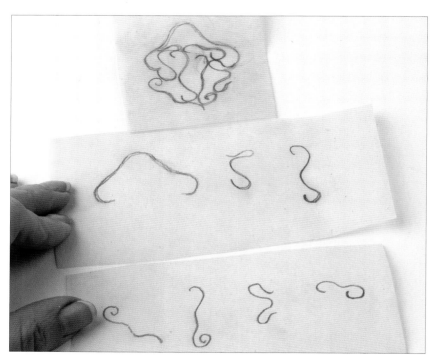

1 Trace the templates given on page 143 on greaseproof paper, or draw out your own design. Take several smaller pieces of greaseproof paper and trace over the individual shapes within the design, spacing them out as shown.

3 Roll each end of the rope with your fingers to make it pointed.

2 Each of the shapes is made separately, so roll out a slim rope of clay to the length required for the first shape.

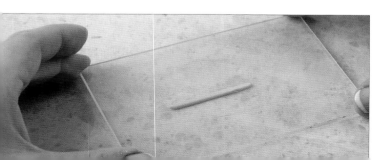

4 Dip your finger in a cup of water and wet the rope of clay. Allow the rope of clay to rehydrate for 30 seconds before transferring it to one of the pieces of greaseproof paper using a paintbrush.

5 Use a wet paintbrush to form the rope into the shape of the coil drawn on the greaseproof paper.

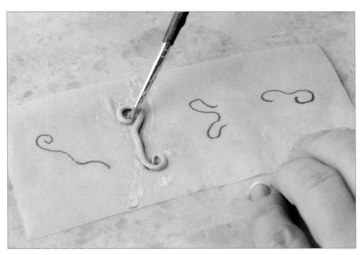

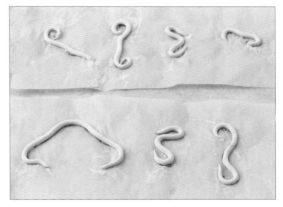

6 Repeat this process of rolling ropes of clay and forming them into coils until you have all the shapes you need.

7 Allow the ropes of clay to dry fully before moving them. When they are dry, they will easily slide off the greaseproof paper. Use a dry paintbrush to brush away any excess dry clay then use a sponge sanding pad to smooth the dry coils. Be very careful when handling them because they are very fragile.

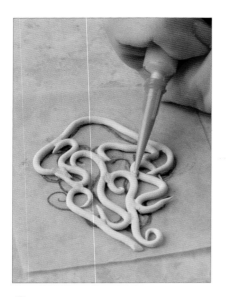

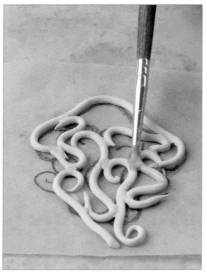

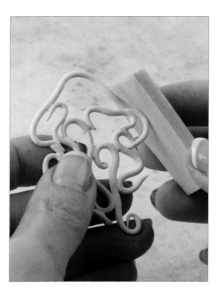

8 Take the piece of greaseproof paper containing your original design and position the coils on top of it to recreate the design. Once you have all the coils placed where you need them, add some silver syringe clay to connect the pieces together.

9 Use a wet paintbrush to seal and smooth the joins and remove any excess syringe clay. Make sure that every join has been sealed.

10 Allow the piece to dry fully. Use a sponge sanding pad or a damp baby wipe to gently smooth any imperfections or rough areas. Be careful because this piece will be very fragile until it is fired.

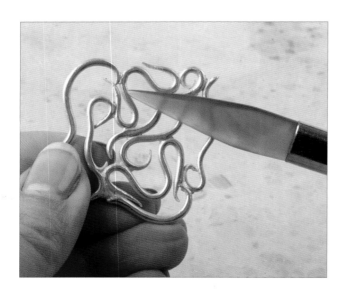

11 Fire the pendant according to the instructions on pages 138–139. After firing, brush the piece gently with a wire brush and polish with an agate burnisher. Attach the pendant to a piece of cord, a choker or string onto a necklace with some beads.

Alternative designs

You can also create matching earrings using the same process; simply attach jump rings and earring findings to the top of each design, and use silver wire to attach a bead at the bottom. Alternatively, create the pendant design from copper or bronze clay for a warmer look.

Adding colour

Although silver, bronze and copper are beautiful precious metals that look lovely in their own right, you may wish to add some colour to your pieces to enhance the metal and bring a new dimension to the design. Here are some interesting ways to bring colour into your work.

Using liver of sulphur

Liver of sulphur is a chemical that can be used to create an antiqued, black or iridescent coloured patina on silver, bronze, copper, gold and other metals. The colours it can create range from gold, copper, blue and purple through to black. This makes it wonderful for creating coloured or darkened effects on your fired pieces of metal clay. Liver of sulphur is also ideal for making any surface texture or decoration more visible, or you can use it to darken findings or chains to give them a vintage look.

1 In a small container, add half a teaspoon of caffeinated instant coffee to hot water and stir well.

2 Add a few drops of liquid liver of sulphur or a small piece of lump form liver of sulphur and mix well.

3 Ensure that your fired metal is brushed and polished; if you are using copper or bronze, ensure that you have pickled the piece to remove any firescale. Prepare for dipping by placing another container of cold, clean water nearby.

4 By suspending the metal clay on wire, or using tweezers, dip the piece into the liver of sulphur solution.

5 Keep submerging the piece in the solution to see the colour of the metal changing.

6 The longer you keep the piece in the solution the more colours will form on the metal. You can also brush the solution onto the metal to pick out individual areas, and then heat it to make the liver of sulphur react.

7 When you are happy with the colour, rinse the piece in cold water to stop the action of the liver of sulphur.

8 You can leave the piece exactly like it is or polish the surface to remove the liver of sulphur from certain areas. The deeper areas of texture will retain the colour.

top tip

The liver of sulphur effects are temporary and will fade or wear off over time. You can add a product such as Renaissance Wax to the surface of the piece to help seal the colour onto the metal and prevent it from fading.

Using polymer clay to add colour

Polymer clay is available in a wide range of bright and bold colours, neutral tones and types with metallic, glittery effects. As it is a clay-like material, it lends itself beautifully to adding precise, bold colour accents.

1 Polymer clay needs a fairly deep base to sit within so you need to plan how your metal clay design will incorporate it. Always fire and brush your piece before adding polymer clay to it.

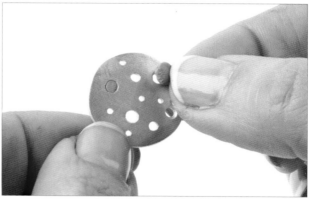

2 Condition the polymer clay first, so that it is soft and malleable, then push the polymer clay into the holes. Smooth it with your fingers to ensure the clay is firmly compacted and fills the holes in the metal.

5 Follow the polymer clay manufacturer's instructions for baking. After baking you can polish the whole piece including the polymer clay. Polymer clay does not shrink after baking but it can sometimes detach itself from the metal. If this happens, use some two-part resin glue or jewellery glue to stick it back in place.

3 Fill all the holes in your piece. Don't be afraid to use different colours – make sure you wash your hands thoroughly every time you change colour to avoid contamination.

4 Cut a circle of polymer clay the same size as your piece and mould it onto the back. Ensure that the edges are firmly smoothed into place. If you have made a hole in the metal for a jump ring to feed through, create a corresponding hole in the clay.

top tip

For colourful, polymer clay jewels, create a bezel within your metal clay piece and add the polymer clay to this after firing.

Using Efcolour enamels

Efcolour is an enamel product that when heated adds a beautiful, glossy colour to metal. This type of enamel is particularly good because it only requires a low level heat, (150°C/302°F) unlike some other enamel products, which require a kiln, or cannot be used on silver because the heating of them would melt the metal.

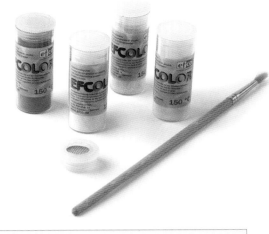

1 Decide upon the design you would like to add to your metal clay. You could apply the Efcolour powder all over the metal, as shown here, or you could use a stencil to create a more intricate design. Brush the surface of your fired piece of metal clay. Do not add any polish to it.

2 Sift the Efcolour powder onto the fired metal clay piece.

3 Use a dry paintbrush to brush away any excess powder, or, if you have used a stencil, carefully remove it trying not to disturb the position of the powder.

4 Place the piece on a baking sheet and bake in a pre-heated oven at 150°C (302°F) for 3–5 minutes to set the enamel.

Using resin to add colour

Resin is a fantastic way to add a colourful flourish to your metal clay designs – when used to fill textures or indentations, as here, it can create a gorgeous, jewel-like effect. Resin is normally colourless, so colouring fluids or pigment powders can be added to it. Resin can also be used as a transparent seal over the top of your creations, which is particularly helpful if you are adding polymer clay to the metal.

1 Wear gloves at all times, as resin can cause skin irritation. Mix the resin according to the manufacturer's instructions. You will only need a very small amount of resin for your metal clay projects.

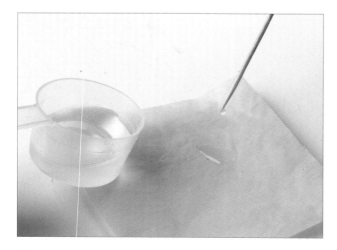

2 Use a cocktail stick to transfer a small amount of resin onto a piece of greaseproof paper.

3 Put a few drops of colouring agent nearby on the greaseproof paper, but keep them separate so that the two do not mix.

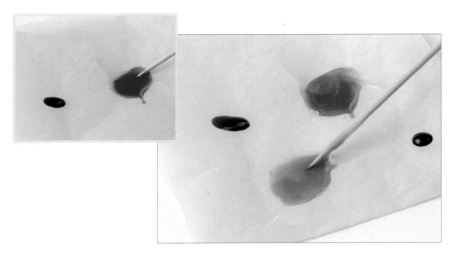

4 Mix a small amount of colour into the resin using a cocktail stick. Gradually keep adding the colour to the resin until you are happy with it. If you would like just a hint of colour and for the resin to be quite transparent, only add a small amount of colour.

5 Apply your coloured resin to the metal a drop at a time, using the cocktail stick to ensure your application is accurate.

6 Allow the resin to cure according to the length of time recommended by the manufacturer. This will be anything from 12 to 24 hours. Place a bowl over your piece while the resin is curing, to prevent any dust from settling on it.

Zebra-print Brooch

Zebra print always seems to be in fashion and looks particularly good as a texture on metal clay. I created my own zebra print rubber stamp when I could not find one. The idea for this project came to me as soon as I pressed the texture into the clay. Adding colour gives this piece another dimension. I have used a bright blue here as the contrast, but experiment with different colours to see which you prefer.

MATERIALS

20g (¾oz) silver clay

Rolling pin

Clay balm

Playing cards

Ruler

Tissue blade

Zebra-print texture sheet

Needle tool

Sponge sanding pad

Silver syringe clay

Small paintbrush

Firing equipment

Wire brush

Agate burnisher

Efcolour enamel in the colour of your choice

Efcolour sieve

Flat nose pliers

Wire clippers

Fine silver brooch fastening

Metal file

1 Roll out a piece of silver clay five playing cards thick. Use a tissue blade to cut out a rectangle shape measuring about 4.5 x 3cm (1¾ x 1¼in). This will form the base of the brooch. Set this aside to dry.

2 Roll out the excess silver clay to a thickness of three playing cards. Press the zebra-print texture into the clay.

3 Use a needle tool to cut out the deepest areas of texture. Be careful not to remove too much clay though – the piece needs to remain intact.

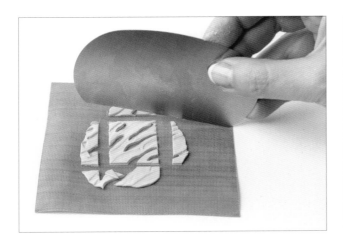

4 Use a tissue blade to cut a rectangle measuring about 4.5 x 3cm (1¾ x 1¼in). Set this aside to dry.

5 After the brooch base and zebra-print piece have dried, sand and smooth them to remove any imperfections. Add some syringe clay to the back of the zebra-print piece and stick this to the brooch base. Add more clay along the stripes to hold them in place if need be.

6 Use a wet paintbrush to remove any excess clay and to seal the join between the two pieces. Apply syringe clay around the outside edges of the brooch so that there is no visible seam where the two pieces have joined. Set the whole piece aside to dry out.

7 After the piece has dried, set the brooch fastening onto the back of the piece. Apply some syringe clay to the parts of the brooch where you would like to set the brooch pin. Use a wet paintbrush to smooth the clay and fully embed the fastenings. Allow the piece to dry.

8 Sand and smooth the back of the piece once more before firing. Fire the brooch according to the instructions on pages 138–139. Allow the piece to cool naturally or quench it in cold water, then brush with a wire brush and an agate burnisher to reveal the silver. Polish the piece or leave it with a brushed finish if you prefer.

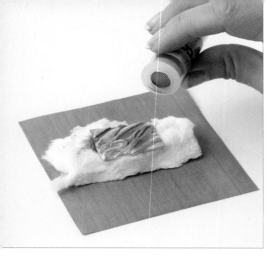

9 Sieve the Efcolour enamel onto the piece, filling the deep ridges in the zebra-print texture.

10 Use a fine, dry paintbrush to brush away excess enamel powder from the surface of the piece. Wherever the enamel powder sits on the metal is where it will melt, so ensure you have placed the powder exactly where you want it to be.

11 Place the brooch onto a baking tray and bake in a pre-heated oven at 150°C (302°F) for 3–5 minutes. Make sure that the piece is completely level during baking. Remove the piece from the oven and check that the enamel has fully melted. Allow the piece to cool before handling.

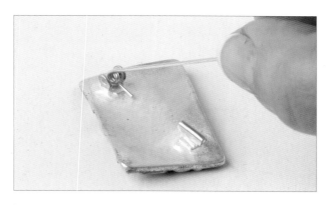

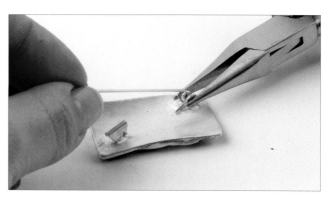

12 Attach the brooch pin to the back of the piece: position the end of the pin inside the pin clasp.

13 Pinch the clasp together with a pair of pliers.

14 If the brooch pin is too long, trim it to the correct length using wire clippers and file with a metal file to sharpen the end of the pin.

Teardrop Gem Art Earrings

Adding colour and texture can bring a piece of metal clay jewellery to life, and gem art granules are the perfect way to do this. These tiny pieces of semi-precious gemstones are a by-product of the gem-cutting industry. After gemstones have been cut to shape and faceted there is a lot of wastage, so these unusable pieces are crushed into small granules. I have found that gem art granules are perfect for adding to metal clay after firing, to give the piece a look of druzy agate. There are many different gemstone varieties and colours, so you will be spoilt for choice.

MATERIALS

10g (¹/₃ oz) bronze clay

Clay balm

Rolling pin

Playing cards

Circle cutter: diameter of about 1.5cm (½in)

Teardrop-shaped cutter: about 2cm (¾in) long

Snake roller

Small paintbrush

Pin vice

Sponge sanding pad

Firing equipment

Pickling equipment

Wire brush

Two-part resin

Cocktail stick

Paper or card

Black spinel gem art granules

Bowl for protection

Flat nose pliers

Round nose pliers

Side cutters

6 bronze-coloured jump rings, 5mm (¼in) diameters

2 bronze-coloured head pins

2 bronze-coloured earring wires

1 Prepare your work surface. Roll out the bronze clay to a thickness of six playing cards. Cut out two teardrop shapes and two circle shapes and set them aside to dry according to the instructions on pages 20–21.

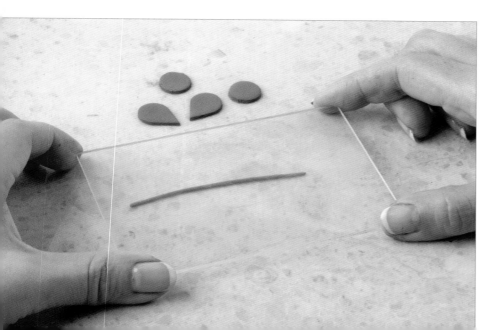

2 Using a snake roller, roll out a thin rope of bronze clay to a length of about 3cm (1¼in). Saturate the rope of clay with water using a wet paintbrush. Allow the clay to hydrate for about 30 seconds.

3 Curl the rope of clay into a teardrop shape and place it on top of one of the teardrop bases. Use a watery paste to seal the join between the rope of clay and the bronze clay base. Repeat this process with the second teardrop shape.

4 Allow the pieces to dry out. Sand and smooth the pieces to remove any imperfections in the dry clay.

5 Drill a hole at the top of each teardrop shape with a pin vice. Drill a hole at the top and the bottom of the two circle shapes. Sand again if necessary. Fire the pieces according to the instructions on pages 138–139.

6 After firing, place the pieces in a hot pickle solution for between 5–30 minutes to remove any firescale. Brush the pieces with a wire brush to bring out the bronze colour.

7 Mix some clear resin according to the manufacturer's instructions. Use a cocktail stick to fill the centre of each fired teardrop shape with resin.

8 Using a folded piece of paper or card for accuracy, sprinkle gem art granules onto the resin – the resin will seep up through the gem granules and secure them in place. Do not worry if the granules fall outside of the centre.

9 Carefully brush away any excess gem granules using a small paintbrush. Be careful not to disturb the pile of granules in the centre of each teardrop – do not worry about being too neat at this stage.

10 Set the shapes aside to cure. Place a bowl over the top of them to prevent any dust from landing on the wet resin.

11 Thread a head pin through each of the teardrop shapes and wrap it around to create a wire loop (see page 35). Use jump rings to attach the bronze circles and the teardrop shapes to the earring wires.

Setting stones

Setting precious and semi-precious stones in your metal clay projects will allow you to create stunning pieces of jewellery with that extra bit of sparkle! Due to the varying properties of gemstones, some can withstand the high firing temperatures of metal clay and others cannot – refer to the charts on pages 140–141 to find out whether your chosen stone can be set before firing, or whether you should fire the metal first and insert the stone after. In this section I will explain how this can be done most effectively.

FACETED STONES

These stones have a pointed base and become wider towards the top. The stone must be set deep enough into the clay so that the clay shrink-locks around the girdle – the widest part of the stone – during firing.

CABOCHON STONES

These stones are domed with a polished surface and a flat base. These must be set deep enough in the clay that the clay shrinks and grips the widest part. These stones look particularly good set into a bezel after firing.

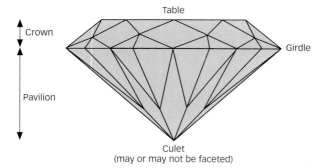

Table

Crown

Girdle

Pavilion

Culet
(may or may not be faceted)

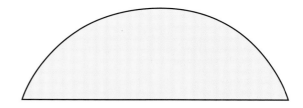

Firing with the stone in place

Check the height of your stone before you start. You'll need to add enough clay to the setting area – or embed the stone deeply enough in thicker clay pieces – to cover the stone's girdle by about 1–2 mm ($^1/_{16}$ in). During firing the metal clay will shrink and lock the stone into the metal.

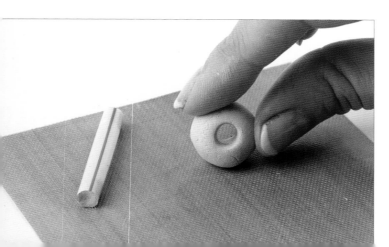

1 Create a ball of clay then push a drinking straw through the centre to create a hole – cutting a hole in the clay under the stone helps minimise the amount that the clay pushes up the stone as it shrinks.

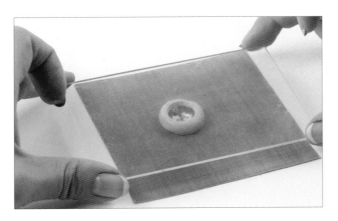

2 Use a hard, flat surface, such as a snake roller, to embed the stone evenly into the clay ball. Ensure that the girdle of the stone is embedded 1–2 mm (¹/₁₆ in) below the surface of the clay, and that the table of the stone is level.

3 Use a circular cutter to trim the edges of the bezel so that you have neat, vertical sides. Attach the bezel to your desired piece of jewellery before firing. After firing, cover the stone with a piece of masking tape before brushing and polishing, to avoid scratching the stone.

CREATING A BEZEL

You can also create a bezel for your stone using a rope of clay. The same rules apply – ensure that the girdle or shoulders of the stone are 1–2mm (¹/₁₆ in) beneath the surface of the clay to allow for shrinkage during firing.

1 Use a snake roller to create a thin rope of clay. Roll the ends of the rope into points using your fingers. Wet the rope with water and allow it to soak for about 30 seconds.

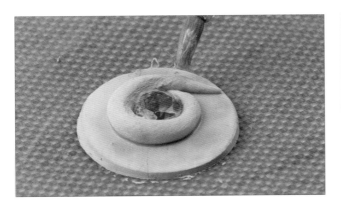

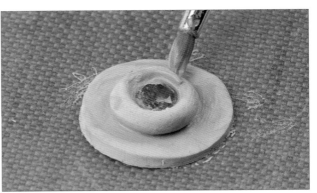

2 Create a base, such as this disc, for your stone to sit on. Using a drinking straw or similar, cut a small hole in the centre before gently placing your stone on top. Use a paintbrush to manoeuvre the rope around the stone, pushing the bezel and stone tightly together.

3 Use the paintbrush to blend the join in the bezel and to seal the bezel to the base. Add some additional syringe clay if necessary. Wipe the stone clean using a baby wipe before you leave it to dry. After firing, cover the stone with a piece of masking tape before brushing and polishing, to avoid scratching the stone.

Adding the stone after firing

Metal clays need to be fired at high temperatures and there are many gemstones that cannot survive the firing process, or being quenched in cold water directly after firing. The perfect solution is to add gemstones after the metal has been fired. This can be done by creating a bezel setting for the stone to sit in, or by creating a 'claw' setting, see pages 110–111.

BEZEL SETTING

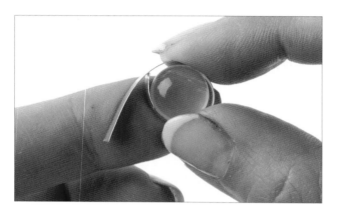

1 Wrap a strip of fine silver bezel wire around your chosen cabochon. There shouldn't be any gaps but the stone should slide in and out of the bezel easily. When you have a good fit, mark the spot where the wire overlaps. Cut it flush, erring on the side of too long rather than too short.

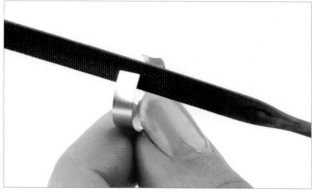

2 File the ends, if necessary, to create a tight seam when the ends are butted together. Check the fit again.

3 Embed the bezel in your wet clay piece – use a flat, hard surface, such as a snake roller, to push the bezel in evenly, being careful not to push it in too deep.

4 Use a small drinking straw to cut a hole through the clay in the centre of the bezel – this will allow light to shine through your stone. Allow the clay to dry.

5 Seal both the bezel join and the bezel's connection to the base piece using silver paste clay. Keep most of the paste on the outside of the bezel so that you don't change the fit. When all the joins are sealed, set the clay aside to dry.

6 Fire the piece and leave to cool. If necessary, file or sand off any excess paste from the outside of the bezel.

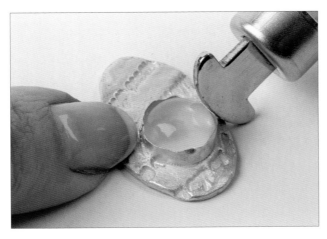

7 Place the cabochon inside the bezel. View the bezel like the face of a clock, and, using a bezel rocker, gently push the bezel onto the stone, first at 12 o'clock then in opposition at 6 o'clock. Repeat at the 3 o'clock and 9 o'clock positions. Work around the stone, pushing the bezel down with opposing movements to keep the stone centred and to prevent the bezel from getting pleated.

8 Place masking tape over the stone to protect it then smooth the pushed bezel with the burnisher by rubbing around the outer edges with a consistent pressure. Give the piece a final polish and it is complete.

top tip

As an alternative to this method, you can seal the bezel wire join with Art Clay Oil Paste before you embed the bezel in the clay. When the join is dry, fire the bezel in a kiln or with a gas torch until the bezel wire joint fuses. File the seam smooth and then embed in fresh clay and follow from step 6 onwards.

WIRE CLAW SETTING

An alternative option is to create a 'claw' type setting by embedding fine wire into the clay before firing. After firing the wire can be bent to hold the stone in place.

1 Take short lengths of wire and bend them so that they are slightly curved. Fold the ends of the wires at 90-degree angles to form 'feet' – these will be embedded in the clay base and securely shrink-locked into place.

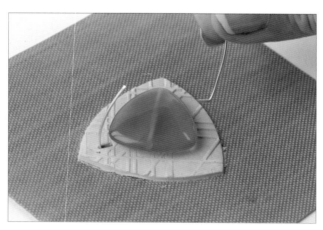

2 So that you can accurately judge the size, place your cabochon on your wet clay base and embed the feet of your wire claws into the clay around the edges of the stone. The wire claws won't shrink, but the clay in which they're embedded will, so leave a little space around the stone to allow for shrinkage.

3 Space the wire claws evenly around the edges of the cabochon stone, then carefully remove it.

4 Seal and strengthen the areas around each 'foot' with paste clay. Use a small paintbrush so that you can apply the paste accurately without spoiling any textures or patterns on your base piece.

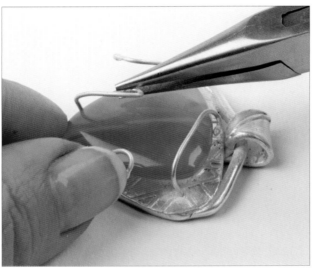

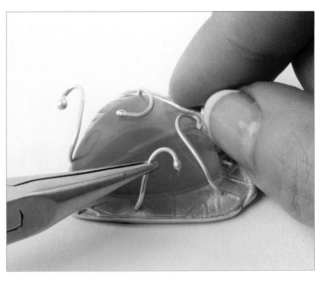

5 After firing, brush the piece to reveal the silver. Place the stone within the claws and gently bend them into place, taking care not to twist them.

6 Ensure that the claws are spaced in an even and pleasing manner, with the ends curled for an extra decorative flourish. Ensure that the stone is completely secure before you wear the piece.

top tip

After firing the piece and before setting the stone, melt the ends of each of the fine silver wires with a gas torch. The heat of the torch melts the ends of the wires into a ball shape, which creates an interesting design feature on this piece. After melting the wires with the gas torch, leave them to cool or quench them in cold water.

Rustic Ring

The true beauty of creating jewellery from clay rather than sheet metal is that you can give your pieces an organic, rustic look much more easily. I love the simplicity and 'ancient' style of this ring – I achieved this by overlapping the join and leaving the edges quite ragged. It is a wide ring so this called for a big gemstone. Do not worry if you don't own a kiln – you can fire gemstones in silver clay that are up to 5mm (¼in) in size using a gas torch or gas stove.

MATERIALS

Ring measuring gauge
Ring sizing papers
Scissors
Wooden ring mandrel
14g (½oz) silver clay
Rolling pin
Clay balm
Playing cards
Any texture stamp
Small paintbrush
5mm (¼in) gemstone
  (suitable for firing in silver
  clay using your method
  of choice – see pages
  140–142)
Snake roller
Circle cutter
Sponge sanding pad
Silver syringe clay
Firing equipment
Masking tape
Wire brush
Silver polish and cloth

1 Measure your finger using a ring measuring gauge. You will be making a ring that is a large width, so you should add four sizes to the ring to allow for shrinkage. For example, if your ring size is 15, you need to make a ring that is size 19. The clay will shrink to a size 15 during drying and firing. Take a ring sizing paper and cut off the excess paper at the cut mark.

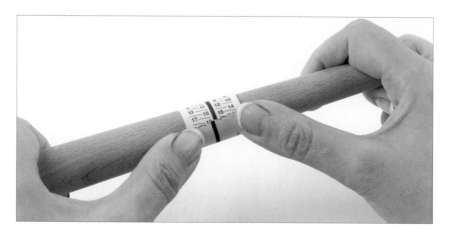

2 Wrap the ring sizing paper around a ring mandrel starting with the non-sticky edge. Adjust the paper until the sticky edge meets the correct measurement line on the paper. Stick the edge down firmly.

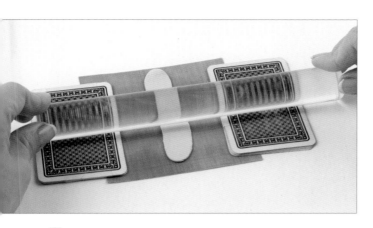

3 Take 10g (1/3 oz) of silver clay and roll this into a strip that is six playing cards thick, approximately 2cm (¾in) wide and long enough to wrap around the ring mandrel and overlap by about 1cm (½in).

4 Apply a light layer of balm onto the texture stamp and press this firmly into the silver clay. Do not trim the clay; an organic, curving edge works best here.

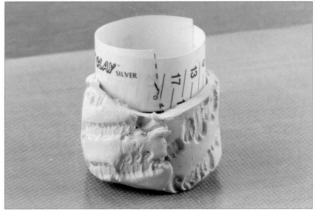

5 Wrap the clay around the ring mandrel where the ring sizing paper is located. Apply some silver paste clay where the ends overlap. Seal the edges of the join with some paste clay and a wet paintbrush.

6 Allow the ring to dry on the mandrel for 30 minutes in a warm place. Gently remove the ring (still attached to the ring sizing paper) and allow it to dry thoroughly according to the instructions on pages 20–21.

7 Roll your remaining silver clay into a ball then press this into a patty shape; it needs to be at least 3mm (¹/₈in) taller than the height of your gemstone. Push the gemstone into the centre of the clay using a snake roller so that it sinks in evenly. The table of the stone needs to be in line with the top of the clay.

8 If necessary, use a small cutter to trim the patty to a neat, straight-sided circle shape. You now have your gemstone set in a silver clay bezel. Remove any clay from the stone using a baby wipe. Allow this to dry.

9 Once the pieces have dried, sand and smooth them to remove any imperfections. Pay careful attention to the inside of the ring to ensure that it feels smooth and that there are no sharp edges where the clay overlaps. If necessary, use some syringe clay to fill these areas and allow to dry once more.

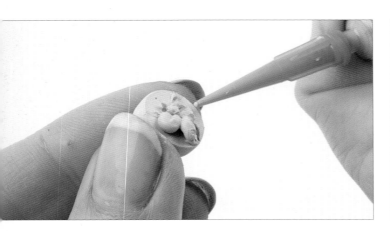

10 Apply a generous amount of syringe clay to the back of the bezel and attach it to the ring.

11 Use a wet paintbrush to remove any excess syringe clay and to seal the join between the ring and the bezel. Allow the ring to dry thoroughly.

12 Fire the ring according to the instructions on pages 138–139. After firing, do not quench the ring in water, but allow it to cool down gently. Apply some masking tape to the stone so that you do not scratch it then brush the ring to reveal the silver. Polish the inside and edges of the ring.

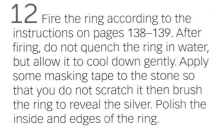

Flower Bracelet with Cabochon

This elegant bracelet design is the perfect way to set a stone after firing. Setting the bezel wire onto two layered pieces of silver clay allows you to embed the bezel into the clay without it weakening the piece or creating cracks at the back. It also means you do not have to roll the whole piece out too thickly, thus saving silver clay.

MATERIALS

Cabochon gemstone (any colour or size)

10cm (4in) fine silver bezel wire

Scissors

Templates (see page 143)

Card

20g (¾oz) silver clay

Rolling pin

Clay balm

Playing cards

Texture sheet of choice

Needle tool or craft knife

Snake roller

Silver paste clay

Small paintbrush

Drinking straw

Sponge sanding pad

Pin vice

Firing equipment

Wire brush

Masking tape

Bezel rocker

Curved metal burnisher

Metal polish and cloth

Round nose pliers

Flat nose pliers

Side cutters

40cm (15in) beading thread

4 silver crimps

4 silver crimp covers

Silver clasp

26 aventurine top-drilled drop beads, 1cm (½in) diameter

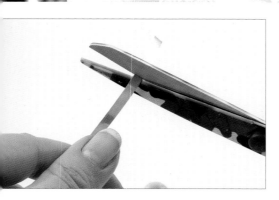

1 Cut a piece of bezel wire to fit around your cabochon gemstone. Follow the instructions on pages 108–109 for preparing the bezel for your design. Cut out a large and small flower template from a piece of card or polythene using the template on page 143.

2 Roll out your silver clay five playing cards thick. Apply a thin layer of clay balm to your texture sheet and press this firmly into the clay.

3 Remove the texture sheet and place the large flower template on top of the clay. Cut around it with a needle tool or craft knife.

4 Roll out the excess clay to a thickness of three playing cards. Place the small flower template onto the clay and cut around it using a needle tool or craft knife. You don't need to apply any texture to this smaller piece.

5 Apply some silver paste clay to the back of the small flower shape and stick it in the centre of the large clay flower. Embed the bezel into the clay through the centre of the small flower. Push the bezel gently into the clay using a snake roller to ensure that the bezel is completely level.

6 Place your gemstone inside the bezel to check that the wire is embedded deeply enough. The bezel wire should sit high enough to cover the shoulders of the stone. Remove the stone and adjust the wire until it is set perfectly. Cut a small hole out of the centre using a drinking straw, and then allow the piece to dry.

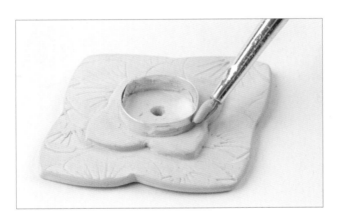
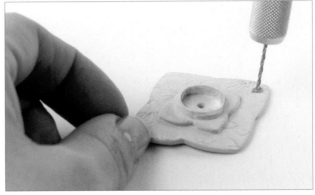

7 After the piece has dried completely, sand and smooth the clay and apply a thin solution of silver paste clay where the bezel meets the silver clay. Seal any gaps inside and outside the bezel to create a strong connection between the wire and the clay. Allow to dry.

8 When the piece is dry, drill a small hole at each end using a pin vice. Fire the piece according to the instructions on pages 138–139.

9 Once the pendant is cool, brush it with a wire brush.

10 Insert the gemstone into the bezel and cover it with some masking tape to prevent it from getting scratched.

11 Set the bezel around the gemstone using a bezel rocker, following the instructions on page 109.

12 Use a curved metal burnisher to smooth and neaten the curve of the bezel around the cabochon.

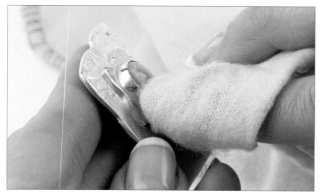

13 Polish the piece so that the metal is smooth and shiny.

14 Attach the bracelet to beads of your choice using some beading thread at each side of the bracelet. Attach a clasp to complete your bracelet.

Hot connections

Although silver, copper and bronze clays all fire at different temperatures, you can still combine them within one piece of jewellery. To do this successfully you should create the piece of metal clay that fires at the hottest temperature first. You can then re-fire this piece with a second metal clay added to it, at a lower temperature. Re-firing the first metal clay will not affect it and the second metal will also be safe.

Overlaying one metal clay onto another

Copper and bronze clays have such a similar colouring (bronze is 90 per cent copper) that it is hardly worth the effort of combining these two metals in one piece of jewellery as there will be very little contrast. On the other hand, silver clay looks beautiful alongside copper or bronze clay – mixing these warm and cool-coloured metals creates a wonderful effect. I find that the designs that work best are those in which the silver clay wraps around or is inserted into the copper or bronze clay.

1 Once you have chosen your design, start by creating the piece of copper or bronze clay that will form the base of your item. Ensure that you roll the copper or bronze clay to a thickness of six playing cards if you have a plain piece or to a thickness of seven playing cards if you are adding a texture. Fire the piece and pickle it to remove any firescale. Brush it with a wire brush to bring out the colour.

2 Roll out your silver clay. When added, the silver clay must overlap the base piece and tightly wrap around it so that when it is fired it will shrink and grip itself in place. Use your fingers to firmly secure the silver clay.

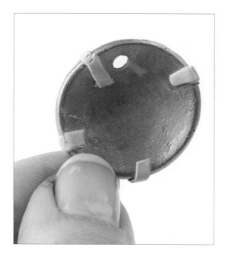

3 Fire the piece again using the methods and timings given for silver clay (see pages 138–139). Brush and polish after firing.

Using plugs

If you want to add just an accent of silver clay to a piece of copper or bronze then this is the best method to use. You will need to create a hole or holes in the piece of metal that is receiving the silver clay, so that the two pieces will 'plug' together. You can either use a pin vice to drill the holes before the clay is fired, or use a drill to create the holes after firing.

1 Make your chosen design from copper or bronze clay: fire the piece and pickle it to remove any firescale. Brush it with a wire brush to reveal the metal.

2 Create a slim sausage-shaped piece of silver clay and feed this through the holes in the fired metal. Ensure that the silver completely fills each hole, without any gaps. Use your fingers to push it firmly into place.

3 Use some silver syringe clay to seal the holes, if necessary. After drying, fire the piece again using the method and timings for silver clay (see pages 138–139). Brush and polish the whole piece after firing.

top tip

This method can also be used for attaching small pieces of silver to the front of the design, using the plug as the connecting join (see pages 122–125).

Copper and Silver Heart Pendant

This simple design illustrates how harmoniously copper and silver can sit alongside one another in a piece of jewellery. This pendant is easy to make and looks delightful strung on a simple silver chain or even a piece of cord. Use the same technique but swap in different shapes if you prefer.

MATERIALS

10g (1/3 oz) copper clay

Plastic wrap

Rolling pin

Clay balm

Playing cards

Large heart-shaped cutter: about 4cm (1½in) long

Tissue blade

Drinking straw

Small paintbrush

Sponge sanding pad

Firing equipment

Pickling equipment

Wire brush

7g (¼oz) silver clay

Small heart-shaped cutter: about 2cm (¾in) long

Baby wipe

Silver syringe clay

Silver polish and cloth

Flat nose pliers

Round nose pliers

Side cutters

51cm (20in) silver chain

2 silver jump rings

Silver clasp

1 Start by preparing your work surface and your copper clay. Condition the clay if it is stiff or crumbly so that it becomes smooth and malleable (see page 19).

2 Roll out a piece of copper clay to a thickness of six playing cards. Cut out a heart shape using the large cutter.

3 Cut a hole out of the centre of the heart, measuring 5mm (¼in) in diameter, using a small drinking straw. Set the heart aside to dry according to the chart on pages 20–21.

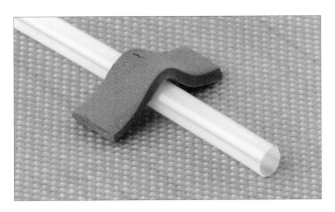

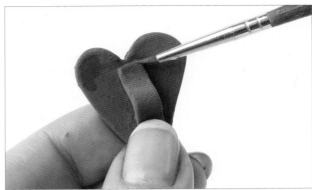

4 Create a bail for your pendant by rolling out a small strip of clay four playing cards thick, 2cm (¾in) long and 5mm (¼in) wide. Trim the sides and the ends. Bend the clay into shape over a drinking straw and leave to dry.

5 Sand and smooth the dried pieces. Mix a little copper clay with some water to create a sticky paste. Apply some paste to the back of the bail and stick this to the back of the pendant. Use a wet paintbrush to remove any excess paste and to seal the join. Leave to dry.

6 After the piece has dried, do any final sanding and smoothing before firing according to the instructions on pages 138–139. After firing, place the pendant in a hot pickle solution for 5–30 minutes to remove any firescale. Brush the piece with a wire brush to reveal the copper.

7 Carefully clean your tools and work surface to prevent cross-contamination of your clays. Roll out a small piece of silver clay to a thickness of three playing cards. Cut out a small heart shape.

8 Create a small sausage of clay and feed this through the hole in your pendant. Use a small paintbrush to ensure that the silver clay fills the hole. Wet the silver plug with water.

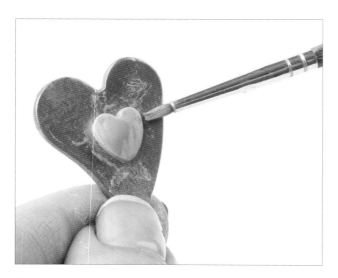

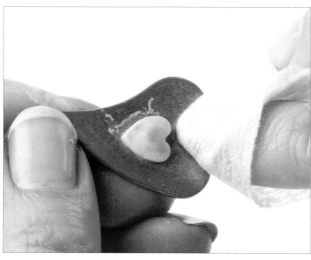

9 Wet the back of your heart and position it on top of the plug. Use a small paintbrush to secure it in place.

10 Clean away any excess silver clay on the copper surface using a damp baby wipe.

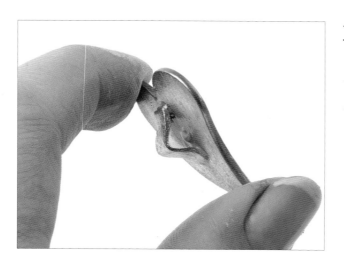

11 Turn the pendant over and add some silver syringe clay to completely seal the hole in the copper. Use a paintbrush to smooth over the hole and remove any excess clay. Allow the silver clay to dry out. When it is dry, gently sand and smooth the clay using a sponge sanding pad.

12 Fire the pendant according to the instructions on pages 138–139. Quench the pendant in cold water to cool it quickly. If firescale has formed you can place the piece in a hot pickle solution to remove it. Brush the piece all over to reveal the silver and polish the central silver heart. Simply thread a chain or piece of cord through the bail to finish.

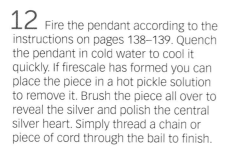

Silver Earrings with Copper Windows

These lovely, dotty earrings combine the elegant qualities of silver with warm copper colours coming through from underneath. You could make these in any shape, using different tools to create your copper 'windows'.

MATERIALS

10g (¹/₃ oz) copper clay
Plastic wrap
Rolling pin
Clay balm
Playing cards
Circle cutter: 2.5cm (1in) diameter
Sponge sanding pad
Pin vice
Firing equipment
Pickling equipment
Wire brush
10g (¹/₃ oz) silver clay
Small and medium drinking straws
Flat nose pliers
Round nose pliers
4 copper-coloured jump rings
2 copper-coloured earring wires

1 Start by preparing your work surface and your copper clay. Condition the clay if it is stiff or crumbly so that it becomes smooth and malleable (see page 19).

2 Roll out the copper clay to a thickness of six playing cards. Cut out two circle shapes using your 2.5cm (1in) cutter. Allow the copper circles to dry out completely, according to the instructions on pages 20–21.

3 After the copper circles have dried, sand and smooth them to remove any imperfections.

4 Drill a hole at the top of each circle using a pin vice – be careful not to drill too close to the edge. Fire the circles according to the instructions on pages 138–139.

5 Place the fired copper pieces in a hot pickle solution to remove any firescale (see page 31). Brush the pieces with a wire brush to reveal the copper.

6 Carefully clean your tools and work surface to prevent cross-contamination of your clays. Roll out a piece of silver clay to a thickness of four playing cards. Cut out two circle shapes using your cutter. Gently press down the edges of the circles to make them slightly larger.

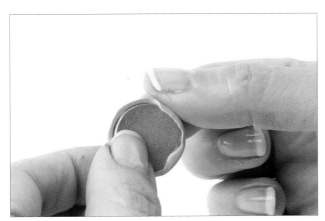

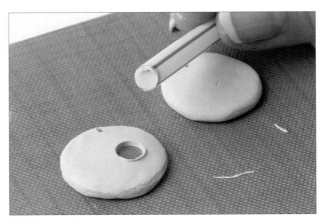

7 Place a silver clay circle on top of each of the fired copper pieces. Press the edges of the silver clay around the copper, so that the silver wraps around the copper snugly and is securely held in place.

8 Use the small and medium drinking straws to make holes in the silver clay. Plunge the straw into the clay to cut the hole, twist the straw and pull it out quickly to remove a small plug of silver clay. This will reveal the copper underneath. Create a random pattern on each earring.

9 Create holes in the silver clay that correspond with the holes you created with a pin vice in the copper. Allow the silver clay layer to dry (see pages 20–21).

10 Sand and smooth the face, sides and back of the earrings to remove any imperfections.

11 Fire the earrings according to the instructions on pages 138–139, then quench them in cold water. Brush and polish the pieces to reveal the silver.

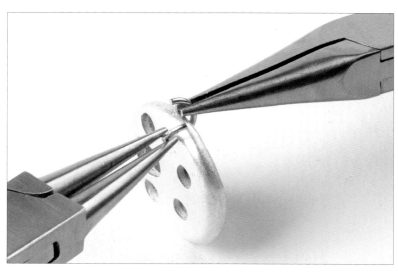

12 Attach jump rings and earring wires to complete your earrings (see page 35).

Finishing touches

As well as being ideal for making entire pieces, such as pendants and earrings, metal clays are also perfect for creating finishing touches. Why not try to create personalised clasps for necklaces and bracelets or even precious metal components for beaded creations? Here are some ideas to inspire you.

Peacock-print Clasp

This clasp is beautiful and very simple to make. It can be used to secure bracelets or necklaces and adds a wonderful design feature to a piece of beaded jewellery. I have used a polymer clay peacock feather texture sheet in this project. You can use any texture you want, either by using a bought texture stamp or by creating your own, see pages 40–43.

MATERIALS

10g (¹⁄₃ oz) copper clay
Plastic wrap
Clay balm
Rolling pin
Playing cards
Peacock feather texture sheet
Tissue blade
Ruler
Small paintbrush
Snake roller
Sponge sanding pad
Pin vice

Firing equipment
Pickling equipment
Wire brush
Round nose pliers
Flat nose pliers
Side cutters
80cm (32in) beading thread
4 copper-coloured beads
4 copper-coloured crimps
4 copper-coloured crimp covers
46cm (18in) strand of peach-coloured pear-shaped beads, 2.5cm (1in) diameter

1 Prepare your clay, conditioning it if necessary (see page 19), then roll it out: roll copper clay to a thickness of seven playing cards; If you are using silver clay, roll it six playing cards thick.

2 Add some clay balm to the rubber texture mat or polymer clay reverse impression and press the texture firmly onto the clay.

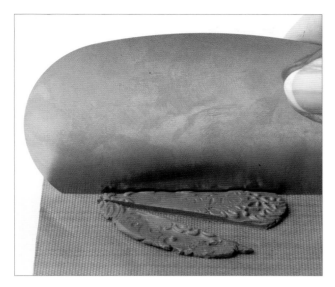

3 Use a tissue blade to cut a strip of clay 4cm (1½in) long – make it 1.5cm (½in) wide at one end, gently tapering to 0.5cm (¼in) wide at the other.

4 Carefully turn the clay over and wet it using a small paintbrush and some water. Allow the clay to soak the water up for a few seconds.

5 Flip the piece so that the textured side is facing up again, and gently bend over about 1cm (½in) of the thin end of the shape to form a hook. Fold a playing card into three and tape it together. Place this under the hook to support it during drying. Allow the clay to dry completely.

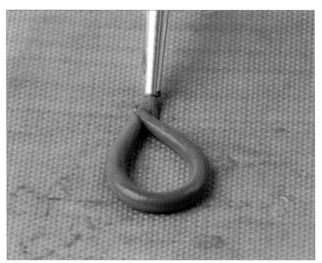

6 Take a piece of excess clay and roll it into a rope 6cm (2½in) long and 3mm (1/16in) thick. Apply some water to the rope using a paintbrush and allow it to saturate the clay for about 30 seconds. To make the eye part of your clasp, form the rope of clay into a teardrop shape. Use the wet paintbrush to seal the ends of the clay together at the top of the shape. Allow the shape to dry.

7 Once both pieces are completely dry, sand and smooth them using a sponge sanding pad. Be very gentle because they will be quite fragile.

8 Using a pin vice, drill two holes at the end of the hook part of your clasp.

9 Fire the pieces according to the instructions on pages 138–139. After firing, place the pieces in a hot pickle solution if you are using copper clay (see page 31). Brush the pieces to reveal the metal colour.

10 Your clasp is now complete. Attach it to a beaded design by adding some jump rings to each component or by running beading thread through the holes in the hook and straight through the eye. Secure with some crimp beads.

Alternative designs

This design also works well in silver: choose beads that coordinate with the tones of the metal, and experiment with different sizes and shapes to create interesting effects.

Geranium Leaf Clasp

Leaves make a wonderful texture for metal clay. Geranium leaves are my particular favourite – not only are they a beautiful shape but they also have a very strong vein that transfers perfectly onto metal clay. This design is a clasp, so can be worn as a pendant that unhooks at the front of the necklace, providing a function as well as being an attractive piece of jewellery.

MATERIALS

- 20g (¾oz) silver clay
- Clay balm
- Rolling pin
- Playing cards
- Fresh geranium leaf, about 3cm (1¼in) wide
- Needle tool or craft knife
- Cocktail sticks
- Sponge sanding pad
- Drinking straw
- Silver syringe clay
- Small paintbrush
- Pin vice
- Needle file
- Firing equipment
- Wire brush
- Agate burnisher
- Round nose pliers
- Flat nose pliers
- Side cutters
- 80cm (32in) beading thread
- 2 silver jump rings
- 2 silver crimps
- 2 silver crimp covers
- 46cm (18in) strand of black facet rice beads, 2.5cm (1in) diameter
- 20 red drop-shaped beads, 1cm (½in) diameter
- 4 black round beads, 8mm (³/₈in) diameter

1 Prepare your work surface. Roll out the silver clay to a thickness of five playing cards and slightly larger than your leaf. Place the leaf face-up on top of the clay. Remove one of the playing cards from each side and roll your rolling pin over the leaf to create a strong impression in the clay.

2 Carefully peel away the leaf. Use a needle tool or craft knife to cut out the leaf shape.

3 Repeat steps 1 and 2 to create a second leaf shape. Use a needle tool to carefully cut out a 1cm (½in) wide semi-circle shape from the bottom edge of one of the leaves.

4 Place cocktail sticks under the leaves to give them a curving, organic shape as they dry, following the instructions given on pages 20–21.

5 After drying, sand and smooth the edges and the back of the leaves with a sponge sanding pad.

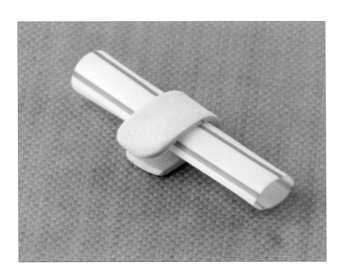

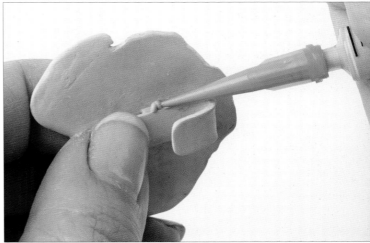

6 Roll out a strip of silver clay three playing cards thick measuring 2.5cm (1in) long and 1cm (½in) wide. Fold the clay over to form a 'C' shape and support this shape with a piece of drinking straw. Leave to dry. This shape will form the hook of your clasp.

7 After the shape has dried, gently sand and smooth it. Use some syringe or paste clay to stick the shape on to the back of the leaf without a hole; position it so that the closed end of the hook points towards the tip of the leaf. Allow to dry out completely.

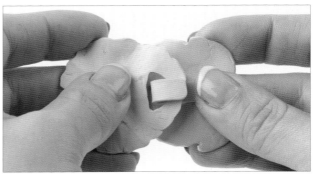

8 Drill a hole in the centre top of each leaf – this is how you will attach the pieces to the necklace. Alternatively, roll a thin rope of clay and create two small, teardrop-shaped loops. These can be dried and attached to the rear of the leaf shapes to provide the starting loops for the chain.

9 Check that the hook and eye of the two pieces fit together well and feel secure.

10 If the hole is not large enough, use a needle file to neatly and carefully enlarge it. Do this gradually and keep checking by inserting the hook.

11 Fire your leaves according to the instructions on pages 138–139. After firing leave to cool or quench in cold water. Brush the leaves with a wire brush to reveal the silver.

12 Polish the edges and the veins of the leaves with an agate burnisher to really make the pieces glisten. Attach a jump ring to each leaf – either through the hole you drilled or the loop you created – and attach the leaves to your beaded design or a piece of chain.

Firing times

Given below are the tried-and-tested firing times and temperatures for every project in the book. Kiln firing copper or bronze clay requires two stages – see the tip box to the right for further information.

Kiln firing

Stage 1: Open fire on wire mesh on a gas stove, or kiln fire at 350°C (662°F) in metal box on top of active coconut shell carbon.

Stage 2: Fire in a metal box; cover piece(s) with a 5cm (2in) layer of active coconut shell carbon.

PROJECT	GAS STOVE	GAS TORCH	KILN
SCRATCH FOAM EARRINGS: SILVER pages 44–47	10 minutes	1.5–2 minutes per piece (Art Clay) 5–10 mins per piece (PMC+ & PMC3)	650°C for 30 minutes 750°C for 10 minutes
SEA URCHIN NECKLACE: COPPER pages 48–51	Cannot be fired using this method	12 minutes (Art Clay) 15 minutes (Prometheus)	Stage 1: 10 minutes Stage 2: 900°C for 60 minutes
SEA URCHIN RING: SILVER pages 52–57	10 minutes	3–5 minutes (Art Clay) 5–10 minutes (PMC+ and PMC3)	650°C for 30 minutes 750°C for 10 minutes
SNAKE BRACELET: SILVER pages 60–63	10 minutes	3.5–5 minutes (Art Clay) 5–10 minutes (PMC+ and PMC3)	650°C for 30 minutes 750°C for 10 minutes
LOVEBIRDS PENDANT: BRONZE pages 64–67	Cannot be fired using this method	12 minutes (Prometheus)	Stage 1: 10 minutes Stage 2: 820°C for 45 minutes
COPPER SET ON PERSPEX PENDANT pages 70–73	Cannot be fired using this method	10 minutes (Art Clay) 12 minutes (Prometheus)	Stage 1: 10 minutes Stage 2: 900°C for 60 minutes
RING WITH INTERCHANGEABLE HEADS: SILVER pages 74–79	10 minutes	3–5 minutes per piece (Art Clay) 5–10 minutes per piece (PMC+ and PMC3)	650°C for 30 minutes 750°C for 10 minutes
MERMAID PENDANT: SILVER pages 82–87	10 minutes	Cannot be fired using this method	650°C for 30 minutes 750°C for 10 minutes
ITALIAN-STYLE PENDANT: SILVER pages 88–91	10 minutes	3–5 minutes (Art Clay) 5–10 minutes (PMC+ and PMC3)	650°C for 30 minutes 750°C for 10 minutes

PROJECT	GAS STOVE	GAS TORCH	KILN
ZEBRA-PRINT BROOCH: SILVER pages 98–101	10 minutes	3–5 minutes (Art Clay) 5–10 minutes (PMC+ and PMC3)	650°C for 30 minutes 750°C for 10 minutes
TEARDROP GEM ART EARRINGS: BRONZE pages 102–105	Cannot be fired using this method	12 minutes per piece (Prometheus)	Stage 1: 10 minutes Stage 2: 820°C for 45 minutes
RUSTIC RING: SILVER pages 112–115	10 minutes	3–5 minutes (Art Clay) 5–10 minutes (PMC+ and PMC3)	650°C for 30 minutes 750°C for 10 minutes
FLOWER BRACELET WITH CABOCHON: SILVER pages 116–119	10 minutes	3–5 minutes (Art Clay) 5–10 minutes (PMC+ and PMC3)	650°C for 30 minutes 750°C for 10 minutes
COPPER AND SILVER HEART PENDANT Part 1: copper pages 122–125	Cannot be fired using this method	10 minutes (Art Clay) 12 minutes (Prometheus)	Stage 1: 10 minutes Stage 2: 900°C for 45 minutes
COPPER AND SILVER HEART PENDANT Part 2: silver centre pages 122–125	5 minutes	1.5–2 minutes (Art Clay) 5–10 minutes (PMC+ and PMC3)	650°C for 30 minutes 750°C for 10 minutes
SILVER EARRINGS WITH COPPER WINDOWS Part 1: copper pages 126–129	Cannot be fired using this method	10 minutes (Art Clay) 12 minutes (Prometheus)	Stage 1: 10 minutes Stage 2: 900°C for 45 minutes
SILVER EARRINGS WITH COPPER WINDOWS Part 2: silver overlay pages 126–129	10 minutes	3–5 minutes per piece (Art Clay) 5–10 minutes per piece (PMC+ and PMC3)	650°C for 30 minutes 750°C for 10 minutes
PEACOCK-PRINT CLASP: COPPER pages 130–133	Cannot be fired using this method	10 minutes per piece (Art Clay) 12 minutes per piece (Prometheus)	Stage 1: 10 minutes Stage 2: 900°C for 45 minutes
GERANIUM LEAF CLASP: SILVER pages 134–137	10 minutes	3–5 minutes per piece (Art Clay) 5–10 minutes per piece (PMC+ & PMC3)	650°C for 30 minutes 750°C for 10 minutes

Firing natural gemstones

Many tests have been done on gemstones and their capacity to endure heat from firing by torch, gas stove and kiln. Research has shown that many gemstones at the highest end of the Moh's scale of hardness can survive firing. Many lab-grown cubic zirconia are also suitable to be fired in place.

When firing copper and bronze clays with a torch it is critical that you quench your pieces in cold water immediately after firing. No gemstone would survive going from such intense heat to cold so quickly, therefore I recommend setting gemstones in your pieces after torch firing copper and bronze clay.

The table below shows the results of tests carried out by metal clay artisans Judi Weers and Kevin Whitmore of Rio Grande, a supplier of metal clay tools and resources in the USA. These charts are only a guide and results cannot be guaranteed. If there is a gemstone that you would like to use and it is not on this list, please do carry out your own further research or tests before firing it in metal clay.

NATURAL GEMSTONES	SURVIVED KILN FIRING AT 650°C (1202°F)	SURVIVED KILN FIRING AT 800°C (1472°F)	SURVIVED KILN FIRING AT 900°C (1652°F)	SURVIVED GAS TORCH (SILVER CLAY ONLY)
AMBER	No	No	No	No
ANDALUCITE	Yes	Yes	Yes	Not tested
APATITE	Yes	Turned white	Turned white	Not tested
BERYL (AQUAMARINE; EMERALD)	No	No	No	Not tested
BLACK SPINEL	Yes	Yes	Yes	Not tested
BLACK STAR SAPPHIRE	Yes	Not tested	Not tested	Not tested
BLUE SAPPHIRE	Yes	Yes	Turned a lighter colour	Yes
CHALCEDONY	No	No	No	No
CHRYSOBERYL (CATS EYE; ALEXANDRITE)	Yes	Yes	Yes	Not tested
DENIM LAPIS	Yes	Not tested	Not tested	Not tested
GREEN MOONSTONE	Yes	Yes	Turned a yellowish colour	Not tested
GREEN TOPAZ	Yes	Yes	Yes	Not tested

NATURAL GEMSTONES	SURVIVED KILN FIRING AT 650°C (1202°F)	SURVIVED KILN FIRING AT 800°C (1472°F)	SURVIVED KILN FIRING AT 900°C (1652°F)	SURVIVED GAS TORCH (SILVER CLAY ONLY)
GREEN TOURMALINE	Yes	Not tested	Not tested	Not tested
HEMATITE	Yes	Not tested	Not tested	Not tested
IOLITE	Yes	Turned a darker colour	Turned a metallic colour	Not tested
LABRADORITE	Yes	Turned milky	Turned milky	Damaged
MOONSTONE (IRID WHITE – TRANSLUCENT)	Yes	Yes	Yes	Not tested
PERIDOT	Yes	Turned a metallic colour	Turned a metallic colour	Yes
OREGON SUNSTONE	Yes	Yes	Turned a lighter colour	Not tested
ORISSA GARNET	Yes	Turned a metallic colour	Turned a metallic colour	Not tested
RAINBOW MOONSTONE	Yes	Yes	Turned an irid-blue colour	Not tested
RED GARNET	Yes	Turned a metallic colour	Turned a metallic colour	Not tested
RHODOLITE GARNET	Yes	Yes	Turned a metallic colour	Yes
RUBY	Not tested	Not tested	Not tested	Yes
STAR DIOPSIDE	Yes	Yes	Yes	Not tested
TANZANITE	Yes	Not tested	Not tested	Yes
TOPAZ (GREEN & WHITE)	Yes	Yes	Yes	Not tested
WHITE TOPAZ	Yes	Yes	Yes	Not tested
TOURMALINE	No	No	No	Not tested
ZIRCON	Yes	Yes	Yes	Not tested

Firing cubic zirconia

Cubic zirconia are gemstones grown in a laboratory and these survive particularly well when fired within silver clay. Not all colours of cubic zirconia retain their original colour so this list is well worth referring to if you are going to kiln fire any cubic zirconia stones within your metal clay jewellery designs.

LABORATORY-GROWN GEMSTONES	SURVIVED KILN FIRING AT 650°C (1202°F)	SURVIVED KILN FIRING AT 800°C (1472°F)	SURVIVED KILN FIRING AT 900°C (1652°F)	SURVIVED GAS TORCH (SILVER CLAY ONLY)
BLACK: OPAQUE	Yes	Yes	Yes	Yes
CHAMPAGNE: TRANSPARENT	Yes	Yes	Yes	Yes
CLEAR: TRANSPARENT	Yes	Yes	Yes	Yes
DARK AQUA: TRANSPARENT	Turned a purple-blue colour	Turned a purple-blue colour	Turned a purple colour	Not tested
DARK BLUE: TRANSPARENT	Yes	Yes	Yes	Yes
DARK RED: TRANSPARENT	Yes	Yes	Yes	Yes
EMERALD GREEN: TRANSPARENT	Turned a brownish-red colour	Turned red	Turned red	Not tested
ORANGE: TRANSPARENT	Yes	Yes	Yes	Yes
PALE LAVENDER: TRANSPARENT	Yes	Yes	Yes	Yes
PURPLE: TRANSPARENT	Yes	Yes	Yes	Yes
RED: TRANSPARENT	Yes	Yes	Yes	Yes
TANZANITE: TRANSPARENT	Turned red	Turned dark red	Turned dark red	Not tested
YELLOW: TRANSPARENT	Yes	Yes	Yes	Yes

Templates

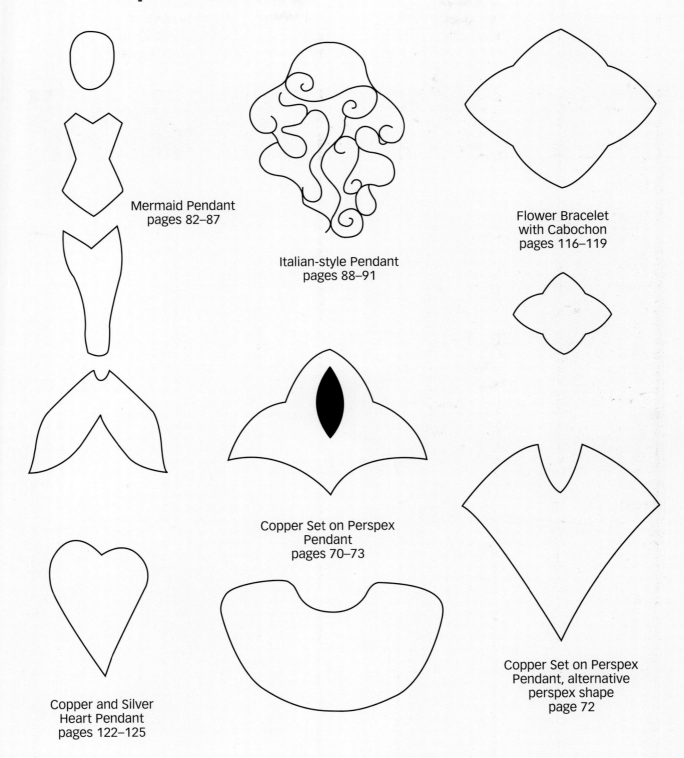

Mermaid Pendant
pages 82–87

Italian-style Pendant
pages 88–91

Flower Bracelet
with Cabochon
pages 116–119

Copper Set on Perspex
Pendant
pages 70–73

Copper and Silver
Heart Pendant
pages 122–125

Copper Set on Perspex
Pendant, alternative
perspex shape
page 72

Glossary

Assay office
A UK institution set up to test the purity of precious metals. Assay offices stamp a hallmark onto items to certify their metallurgical content.

Bail
A component used to attach a pendant to a necklace. The bail is normally placed where the necklace hangs.

Bezel
A rim that encompasses and fastens a jewel, stone or other object into a piece of jewellery.

Cabochon
A stone with a flat bottom with the sides rising up into a dome on the stone's top.

Findings
Components that connect pieces of jewellery together such as jump rings, head pins, earring wires and clasps.

Firescale
A reddish-brown crust that appears on copper and bronze pieces when they are fired and the metal comes in contact with oxygen.

Oxidisation
The action of oxygen on copper and bronze when the metals are heated. Oxidisation creates colour changes in the metals.

Pickle
Pickle is a solution used to remove oxidisation and other impurities from the surface of metals such as sterling silver, copper and bronze. A pickle is an acid bath, and, in some ways, is similar to the brine used to pickle vegetables.

Sintering
The welding together of small particles of metal by applying heat below the melting point.

Supplier

I'd like to thank **Jewellery Maker TV** who kindly supplied me with metal clays and gemstones.
www.jewellerymaker.com
telephone: 0800 6444 655

Index